A Sender's Guide to Letters and Emails

A Sender's Guide to Letters and Emails

Chandana Kohli

hachette
INDIA

First published in 2013 by Hachette India
(Registered name: Hachette Book Publishing India Pvt Ltd)
An Hachette UK company
www.hachetteindia.com

SRD

ISBN 978-93-5009-764-9

Hachette Book Publishing India Pvt. Ltd
4th & 5th Floors, Corporate Centre

Plot no. 94, Sector 44, Gurgaon 122003, India
Typeset in Arno Pro by
Eleven Arts, New Delhi

Printed and bound in India by
Manipal Technologies Limited, Manipal

FSC
www.fsc.org
MIX
Paper from
responsible sources
FSC™ C104740

Contents

PART II: PERSONAL LETTERS

Introduction

Why Read this Book?

In today's fast-paced world, everyone is in a hurry. Social networking is the norm on the go and so is writing a letter. An SMS is what the earliest letter was – a message sent off to inform, to show displeasure, shower greetings, display affection and it is sent in a matter of a few seconds to get the basic idea across. For more complex requirements, there is the email. Although the medium might have changed, the letter is no less important as it was in the ancient times. In fact, we write many more letters today as communication has emerged as an all-important tool for facilitating business as well as social interactions. And every time we sit down to the frame that difficult letter about a possible raise to the boss, or try and write a heartfelt mail to the close friend who has just been through a divorce, we find ourselves struggling. Composing a good email requires as much thought and attention as a formal physical letter that is sent by post. Those foundation English classes in letter writing back in middle school hardly prepare us for the real adult world where a wrong term could ruin your professional career and an incorrect tone could destroy a relationship.

This book is a guide to effective communication in the workspace as well as in your personal lives and will enable you to master the **3 Es** –

EFFICIENCY

Writing that perfect letter suited to the occasion even when pressed for time.

EFFECTIVENESS
Writing an effective letter that will yield the desired response quickly.

ENTERPRISE
Taking initiative and having a ready response for different kinds of situations.

A Sender's Guide to Letters and Emails for all Occasions is an attempt to suit all your requirements both professional as well as personal and provides you with samples and templates of letters that you can easily adapt to your requirements. It is also a manual that will help you become proficient at writing letters and emails of all kinds and provide you with invaluable tips on style, language and form.

This book is a letter writer's resource and assistant that will enable you to write letters efficiently and quickly and effectively, getting your message across in the clearest way possible. The book will tell you when to write a simple email and when to send a message across as a formatted letter attachment or by physical mail as well as quick tips on how to convert a letter into an email.

So why wait to be daunted by the task of writing a letter, just flip through the pages and pull out your sample. All you need to do is remember to replace the names!

A Brief History of Letter Writing

THE EARLIEST LETTERS

Letter writing is an art. It is the oldest form of communication that goes back thousands of years. Before the technological development in communication, handwritten letters were the only means of correspondence. In ancient Egypt, people used to write letters to their dead ancestors seeking their blessings and guidance whenever they were in trouble. Some of these letters were written on bowls found inside the tombs. The Bible includes a series of letters written by Paul the Apostle which were called the Pauline Epistles. They are an integral part of the New Testament. A lot of our knowledge of history has been reconstructed through extensive research on old letters as in most cases they were the only records available.

LETTER WRITING AS A SKILL

During the 19th century in England letter writing became an important medium to express feelings and sentiments as well as to convey important messages or make an announcement. According to the etiquette manuals which were extremely popular in this period, the mark of an accomplished lady lay in her letter writing skills. The educated upper classes had to cultivate the art of penmanship and letters had to be elegantly written and impeccable in the style and language that they used.

STATIONERY

The choice of stationery was equally important in making a good impression. Coloured paper embossed with flowers in the corner was commonly used in the 19th century and was the paper of choice for personal letters. Subsequently, only heavy, white or cream-tinted plain paper was considered suitable. Monogrammed stationery became popular during this period.

SENDING LETTERS

Although all it takes to send a letter today is the click of a mouse or a button on a smart phone, back in the day when there was no technology, sending letters was a complicated process. In the ancient times, letters were dispatched through messengers who physically ran with them from the sender to the recipient. For a long time, mail was only a machinery of governments, armies and kings and a means to send important messages during times of war. In the 6th century BCE, the Persian Empire developed a relay system to send mail that could cover up to 100 miles a day; when horses got tired, they were traded for a fresh one at the different posts that were set up. The Greeks, typically, employed athletes and trained runners to deliver their mail – Philonides, courier and surveyor for Alexander the Great, once ran from Sicyon to Elis – a distance of 148 miles in one day! Augustus Caesar had a relay similar to the Persians, with stopping points – or 'post houses' – where couriers could rest and trade horses. But after the Roman Empire fell, the mail network collapsed, and so did organized communication throughout Europe. During the medieval period, homing pigeons were used for sending letters. This service known as pigeon post, took advantage of the singular quality of this bird, which when taken far from its nest, was able to find his way home due to a particularly developed sense of orientation. Messages were then tied around the legs of the freed pigeon, and it would fly back home where the recipient could read his or her letter.

The development of the modern postal system can be traced to the mid-19th century in England under Sir Rowland Hill who came up with the concept of prepayment through postage stamps. The postal system began to grow and also became a nationalized service under governments across the world and even contributed to the development of roads and transport systems as they had to send mail to the far corners of the country.

THE INDIAN POSTAL SERVICE

In India, the postal services grew over a span of centuries starting from the time of Chandragupta Maurya (322–298 BCE). However, a more systematic communication network was developed during the Mughal era.

The postal services as we know it today was initiated mainly by the East India Company and it was known as 'Company Dawk'. In 1688, the first post office was established in Mumbai and Madras. The first Indian Post Ofice Act came into effect in 1854 and adhesive stamps were introduced on 1 October 1854, on an all-India basis. Indian postal stamps depict the important historical events along with the heroes of the country which include patriots, great leaders, educationists, saints and other people and events which have made India proud.

MODERN MAIL

The development of the Internet and the growth of email has reinvented letter writing and communication services, making it simple, efficient, quick and extremely accessible. However, this has not led to a decline in the use of postal mail. Official letters, cheques, mailers, ad brochures continue to be sent by post as email addresses are an extremely private thing. In India especially, the poor Internet penetration outside of the main urban centres and the lack of education makes the postal system extremely important as a means of reaching the farthest interiors of the country. Post offices in the rural areas of India often act as banks, information centres and government offices rolled into one. It is no wonder that the Indian postal network is the largest in the world with 55,015 post offices across the country.

THE EVOLUTION OF THE LETTER

The nature of writing has been constantly evolving, particularly due to the development of new technologies over the centuries. The pen, the printing press, the computer and the mobile phones have been the latest technology in each successive era and have altered the format of letters and the medium through which it is sent.

The advent of the Internet and the growth of email as well the proliferation of computers and smart phones have turned the letter digital and the sending of it requires no more than a single click.

The characteristics of letters have changed over the years. The language has become simpler and more precise and some colloquial expressions are also included at times. Instead of writing long elegant letters in a formal language, the economy of words seems to have become a practice. Clarity and brevity are the most important aspects of modern-day letter writing. Written communication can be transmitted through emails or SMSs making the above-mentioned values extremely important.

The changes in technology have led to a substantial growth in the number of letters we write today. Both in the work space and at home, shooting off an email is often easier and quicker than actually talking to a friend, colleague, or business acquaintance over the phone or in person.

TYPES OF LETTERS

Letters are generally categorized into two broad types – **Business Letters** and **Personal Letters**. Business letters are basically informative, formal and concise and serve a specific purpose. They are regulated by certain rules and norms. They are goal-oriented. To maximize the impact of the business letter, it should be precise and explicit – it should state its message at the outset clearly and have a positive approach. Technical jargon should be avoided as far as possible in business letters and the message should be simply stated. Effective communication is very important for the organization's business development. Business communication requires focusing on the objective of the letter.

Personal letters are informal and usually exchanged between friends or well-acquainted people to express personal feelings or to inform about social matters. There is no convention for a personal letter like there is in the business letters. It does not require formal concise language – it depends on the relationship and familiarity between sender and recipient.

SIGNIFICANCE OF EMAIL

Email is the abbreviated form of Electronic Mail. It has redefined the very notion of mail and created an entirely different way of high-speed communication. Emails enable instant data transfer and this is the reason for its extensive use as a highly effective communication tool in today's world. Messages are sent and received with or without attachments for speedy communication and can be transmitted to any part of the world within minutes. The email allows quick feedback and fast response to clients' enquiries. As a result, it helps to increase productivity and also saves a significant amount in postage cost. All that it takes to send an email is a working Internet connection between the sender and the recipient and a computer, tablet or smart phone to send/receive it on. In short, the email has made communication easy, effective and instantaneous.

The Basic Format of a Business Letter

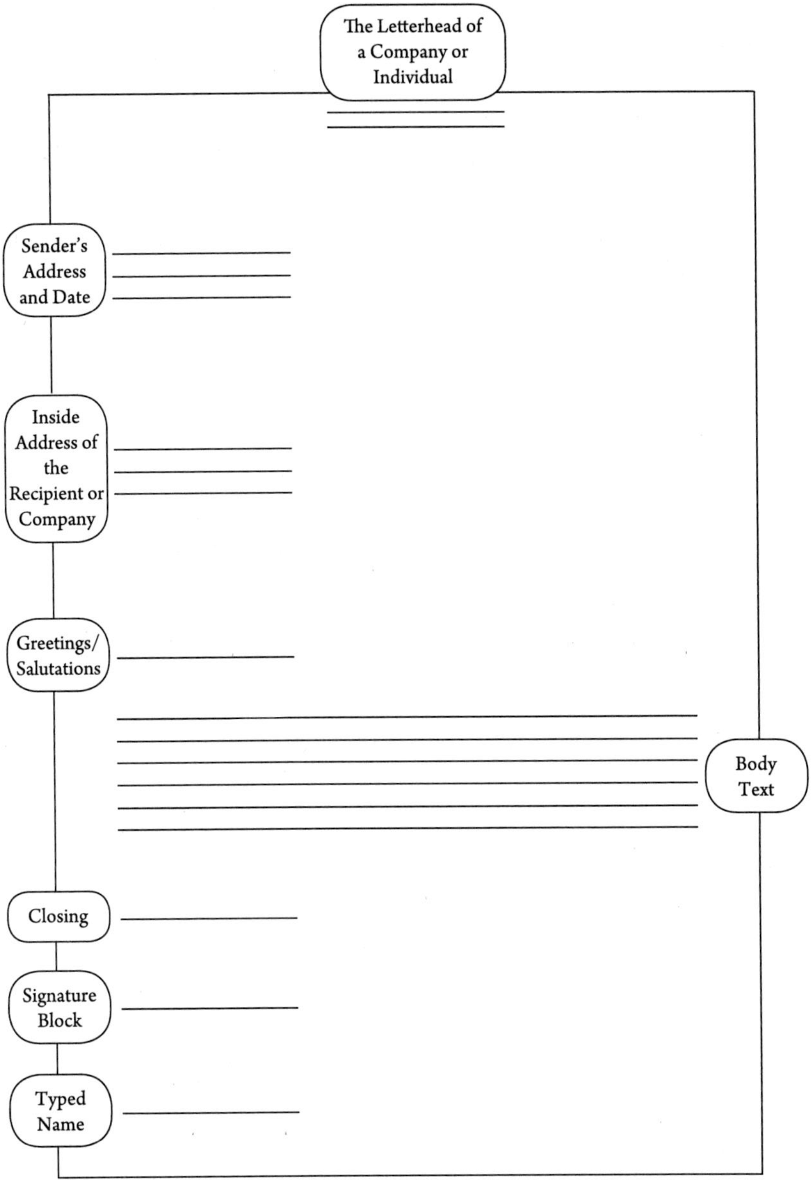

The Basic Format of a Business Email

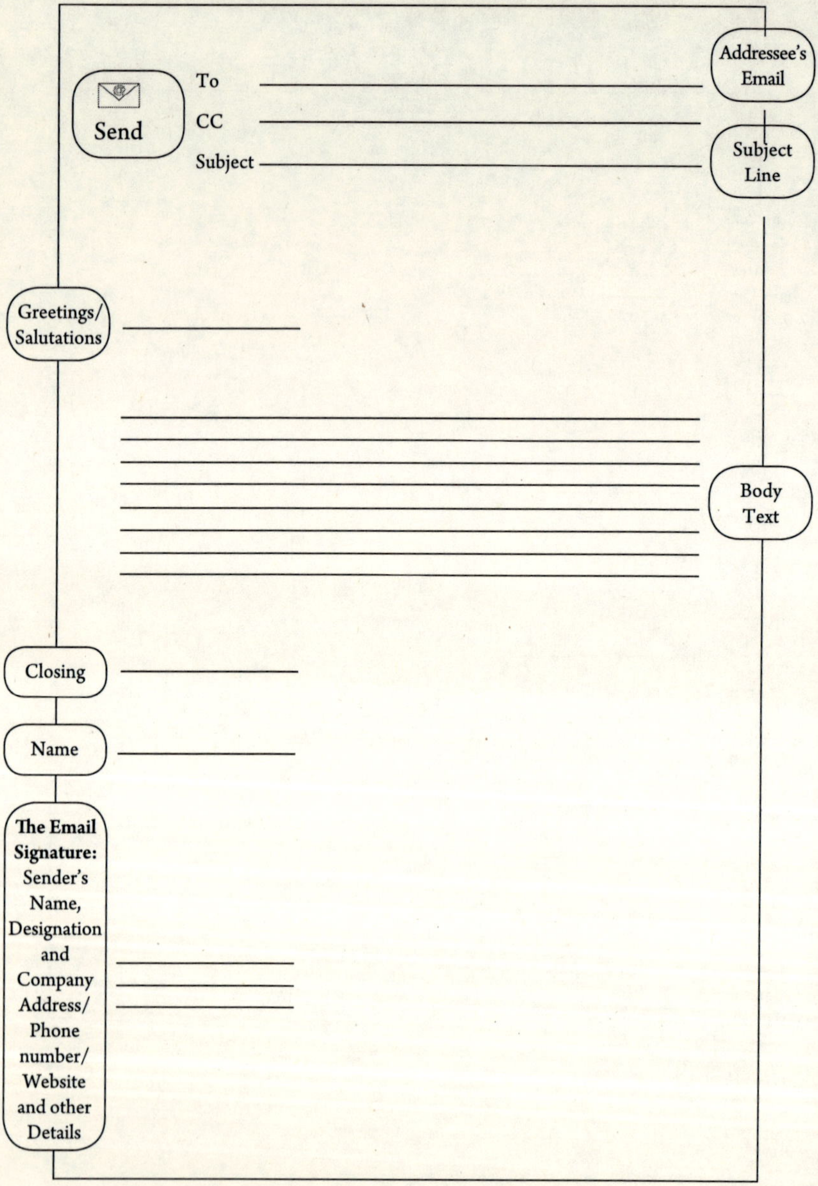

PART I

Business Letters and Formal Letters

Types of Business Letters

A business letter is used for intra-organizational as well as inter-organizational communication. This kind of correspondence is also used to communicate between individuals and organizations. There are a whole range of business letters written for a variety of reasons and purposes.

Official Letters are used for communication within a work space and with its related vendors and clients. Application Letters and Cover Letters are extremely important documents written by a job applicant that can affect the candidate's chances at procuring an interview, or even the job. Bank Letters address important issues with billing and account details and are valuable as evidence of any error on the bank's part. Complaint Letters are also extremely important as they show an error on the part of an organization or service provider and help correct the oversight or mistake. Other business letters include Enquiry letters, Legal Letters, Customer Service Letters, Letters to Government Bodies, Recommendation and Reference Letters and many, many more.

The style and tone of the letter depends on the nature of the relationship between the concerned parties—the sender and the addressee and the basis or reason behind the letter. Business letters should always be typed out and have a formal language and tone as they are used as permanent records and evidence of intent.

Tips on Writing Effective Business Letters

- **Focus** – the purpose of the letter should be clearly outlined and the main theme of the letter should be clear to the reader.
- **Language** – it is better to use simple and direct language and avoid all kinds of jargon except when it is required to describe a technical product.
- **Information** – letters should be informative and depict a complete picture of the specific purpose or main objective. Unnecessary data and details may confuse the reader and should be avoided.
- **Positive Approach** – letters written with a positive touch receive better attention from the recipients than threatening or rude letters.
- **Accuracy** – there should be an emphasis on accuracy. This includes gramatical mistakes, errors in structure, spellings, facts and figures. Mistakes in any of these aspects affect the credibility of the writer and as a result, the purpose of the letter is somewhat lost.
- **Length** – business communication should always be short and precise. It should include all the necessary information and details without making it unnecessarily long. Elaborate letters at times distract the reader from the main topic.
- **Repetition** – avoid any repetition as a letter should be brief and repeating the same points will just irritate the reader.
- **Format** – a standard format is usually acceptable for the business letters. Keep in mind that it should look neat and

presentable. A business letter should be typed in a clear and legible font in 10–12 point size. The standard letter paper size was traditionally 8 inches × 10.5 inches. However, today, the A4 paper size has become the norm for most letters.

- **Salutation** – standard business salutations should end with a comma:
  Dear Sir,
  Dear Mr Doe,
  Dear John,
  Dear Mr John Doe,
- **Close** – standard business closes have the first word in upper case and end with a comma:
  Yours sincerely,
  Yours faithfully,
  Best regards,
  Warm regards,
  Thanking you,

Business Communication Via Email

Modern-day business letters are sent both as hard copies and as emails. While we can attach the word document to the email, this is sometimes not advocated as formats and software versions used by the sender and receiver might be different. Also, many organizations are averse to opening attachments from outside their server and this might affect the future of the letter in question. One way to get around this is to paste the contents of the business letter into the body of the email without changing anything apart from the address lines. Keep the following points in mind while sending out business emails:

- The email should be no different from snail mail and should retain all the information in the printed letter apart from the actual signature.
- Do not write reams as an email is read on various platforms and a very long letter is hardly readable on a smart phone.
- Always have the hard copy of the business letter to use as a reference to draft out the email.
- Certain letters like job offers, acceptance, resignation, promotions, contractual letters and anything which could have a legal use, or function as a reference in the future, should be retained as hard copies with signatures vis-à-vis a simple email. This is because a business letter with a signature has a greater legal standing and can be used to clarify any doubts or disputes.

- A business email is a formal document and make sure that you treat is as such and not like a casual letter as it carries equal importance in an official set-up.
- Do not attach documents unless specifically mentioned and do not use outdated or unusual formats.
- The letterhead or sender's address and date line on top can be eliminated. This part is not required as most official emails have a signature line with the company address and telephone numbers. If you are sending a business email from a personal address then you can put your address at the bottom left corner after your name.
- Proofread your email even if it is short and sent via a phone as typos are just signs of carelessness.
- Do not spam any organization by sending multiple copies of the same mail.
- The subject line of the email should be specific so that it gives the recepient an idea of the contents of the mail.
- Appropriate greetings and sign off – the recipient should be addressed appropriately before starting the mail. At the end of the email, the name, designation and the name of the organization should be mentioned in case there is no company signature.
- Messages should be formatted for easy reading with a standard font in legible size.

Official Letters

Official letters are used for communication within a workspace and between employers and employees of an organization. These kinds of letters can be broadly divided into two parts: letters from employers and letter from employees to employers. This type of letter is extremely important and should be drafted with care as it is representative of a particular organization's ethos and should be written with that in mind. Senior members of the company should be aware of their responsibilities and should correspond with their subordinates accordingly.

Employers write achievement letters to employees to acknowledge their outstanding performance, to boost their morale and to inspire a better performance in the future. Letters related to performance evaluation, promotions and job transfer also form a routine part of day-to-day administration. These are formal letters sent to the employees and copies of these letters go to the employees' personal files for keeping of records and future reference. Letters about employee misconduct, warning letters and termination letters are important official letters and give employees a reason for a poor bonus payout or being laid off. These letters should specifically mention the facts accurately and be short and to the point.

Intra-office mails to all employees are sent via circulars and are issued to communicate information and important business news to a number of people simultaneously. Internal circulars are meant for employees only and deal with organizational affairs such as holidays, bonus, overtime and salary revision, among others. Circulars should never convey confidential matters and should be simple and precise.

Business memoranda are inter-office correspondence sent between employees, to communicate ideas, convey decisions and to make announcements. They are less informal than business letters and include all important aspects of the topics they relate to.

Other official letters deal with issues of resignations, recommendations, requests and appraisals. Employees can also write to the higher authorities in an organization voicing their displeasure and complaining about sexual harassment and poor work environment. These letters should specifically mention the facts.

It is extremely important to remember that these letters can be preserved for future reference and traced back to the sender at any given point in time. Hence, the tone should always be formal, businesslike and should not compromise the sender or the reader in any way.

1. LETTERS OF ACHIEVEMENT

A letter of achievement is generally issued to someone to acknowledge their outstanding performance and sincere efforts. It is a form of appreciation from the higher authorities in a company. This kind of a letter can also be issued by the senior management of the company to their business counterparts for any outstanding achievements or awards. The tone should be congratulatory and the following points should be kept in mind:

- Language should be simple and sincere
- Tone should be uplifting and morale boosting
- The message should be inspirational and encouraging

a. Personal Achievement Letter

Sample:

Company Letterhead

Date

Mr Krishna Kant Sahai
Project Manager
Eastern Cement Company Limited
24, Lal Bagh
Patna – 200 001

Dear Sir,

We are writing this letter to recognize your extraordinary effort and hard work for the success of the Darbhanga Project. You went above and beyond your duties to achieve this important target. Your enthusiasm and ability to motivate your colleagues has showed in a significant increase in productivity of the company.

Your team under your able guidance and leadership put as much hard work and dedication into this project and the results you accomplished were a real boon for the company. With you on this project, our company has reached a new height of success. Through the feedback from our clients, it is evident that your contributions were the main reason behind this project's timely and successful completion.

We once again want to thank you for your brilliant work and we hope that you continue putting in a similar performance for the Eastern Cement Company's better future

Best regards,

Signature

(Mridul Kumar Singh)
Director (Projects)

To: krishnakant.sahai@easterncementindia.com
Subject: Congratulations for Good Performance

Dear Sir,

We are writing this letter to recognize your extraordinary effort and hard work for the success of the Darbhanga Project. You went above and beyond your duties to achieve this important target. Your enthusiasm and ability to motivate your colleagues has showed in a significant increase in productivity of the company.

Your team under your able guidance and leadership put as much hard work and dedication into this project and the results you accomplished were a real boon for the company. With you on this project, our company has reached a new height of success. Through the feedback from our clients, it is evident that your contributions were the main reason behind this project's timely and successful completion.

We once again want to thank you for your brilliant work and we hope that you continue putting in a similar performance for the Eastern Cement Company's better future

Best regards,

Mridul Kumar Singh

Email Signature Line

b. Congratulations to Employee

Sample:

Company Letterhead

Date

Mr Arvind Tewari
Project Manager
Bridge Construction Company Ltd
Sector V
Salt Lake City
Kolkata – 700091

Dear Mr Tewari,

Please accept our heartiest congratulations on behalf of the company for winning the award of 'Star Performer of the Year'. Your performance has been really outstanding throughout the year and is a reflection of your sincere work, perseverance and diligence.

The company appreciates your proficiency, your positive attitude and your interaction with your team members and juniors. Your team has excelled under your able guidance.

All of us at Bridge Construction Company extend our best wishes for your future achievements.

Yours sincerely,

Signature

Nilesh Shah
Director (Human Resources)

c. Congratulations to Customer/Business Associate (Corporate)

Sample:

Company Letterhead

Date

Mr Dhiraj Kumar Saxena
Managing Director
Sun Consumer Products Limited
24, Barakhamba Road
New Delhi 110 001

Dear Mr Saxena,

We are delighted to know that your company's name has been chosen for the award 'Best Manufacturer of Consumer Products' by the Chamber of Commerce for the year 2013. Congratulations on your splendid achievement in winning this award. Your company's outstanding contribution and commitment is felt by all within the industry.

The award is more significant as it supports the generous work you do regarding donation and providing service to the underprivileged sections of the society. Your company's name is on the top of the list of corporate contribution towards social causes.

Congratulations once again and wish you all the best for future achievements.

Warm regards,

Signature

Narinder Singh
Chief Operating Officer

d. Letters of Accomplishment (Corporate)

A letter of accomplishment is generally issued by the company to other corporate houses, competitors as well as group companies and senior shareholders to inform them of results. These results are based on facts and figures marking achievements and growth in the market as well as excellence of any product or marketing campaign.

The tone here should be:

- Precise
- Formal
- Accurate
- Facts and figures should be mentioned indicating the accomplishment of the company

Sample:

Company Letterhead

Date

Mr L.P. Singh
Chairman
Eastern Engineering Company Ltd
22, Dalhousie Junction
Kolkata – 700 001

Dear Sir,

Annual Report for 2010–11

The Eastern Engineering Company's Annual Report has been finalized and it will be published shortly. I would like to apprise you of the corporate performance during the current financial year. The company has reached its projected target of 10% growth in business which has exceeded our expectations.

During the year under review, the company's revenue has increased by 8.6% over last year to reach ₹ 2,000 crore – the overall increase in total income was 7.7%.

We have achieved a substantial reduction in the operational cost of the company and in several categories it was more than our projected target.

This reflects that the corporate performance during the year has improved considerably. This enormous achievement has been realized despite very serious challenges in the market. The company looks forward to the opportunity of fulfilling its objective of being a viable and innovative concern in future. The credit for this success goes to our employees for their support, initiative and good work.

The company has earned recognition from various government bodies for the successful completion of its several turnkey projects.

We look forward to a productive and prosperous new year.

Yours faithfully,

Signature

Anil Kumar Sen
Managing Director

2. LETTERS OF ADJUSTMENT

These letters should be simple and clearly apologetic excusing the company's oversight in the matter at hand. The customer must be placated and the representatives of the companies should offer compensation to make up for the error. The letter should be:

- Apologetic
- Polite
- Clear and the compensation must be clearly mentioned as this letter could be used as proof in later disputes if any

Sample:

Company Letterhead

Date

Mr G.K. Garg
111, Taratala Road
Kolkata – 700 027

Dear Sir,

Please accept my apology for the incorrect shipment of OTG Ovens and the delay in reshipping the order. It was our mistake.

The 300 Deluxe OTG Ovens (Ref. # XT111) that you originally ordered were shipped out freight-free today. You should receive them tomorrow via UPS overnight Blue Dart delivery.

In addition, as there is no excuse for the delay and inconvenience, I have instructed our Finance Department to credit your account with an amount of ₹ 5,000. This reflects the 10% discount routinely applied to orders larger than ₹ 50,000.

We regret that this has happened and hope the actions we have taken make up for it. We value your long years of association with us and want to continue to serve you in the future. If there is anything else we can do, please do not hesitate to call.

Yours faithfully,

Signature

Frank Thompson
Customer Service Manager

3. LETTER OF CASH ADVANCE

As this is a request letter. The letter should be:

- Brief
- Formal
- Confident
- Persuasive

Sample:

Company Letterhead

Date

Mr M.S. Suri
Manager (Finance)
Bell Timber Works
33, Syed Pir Avenue
Kolkata – 700 077

Dear Sir,

I would be grateful if you please sanction me an advance of ₹ 50,000 against my salary for my daughter's wedding to be held next month.

In consideration of the company granting me the advance, I hereby undertake to repay the advance in 10 monthly installments of ₹ 5,000 each.

I also hereby authorize the company to deduct the monthly installment from my July 2013 salary payable on 1 August 2013.

In the event I leave the employment of the company for any reason whatsoever before the full repayment of the advance, I hereby authorize the company to settle the unpaid amount from my retirement benefit dues.

Thanking you,

Signature

Rameshwar Singh
Chief Clerk (Projects Division)

To: marutsundar.suri@belltimberindia.com
Subject: Request for Cash Advance

Dear Sir,

I would be grateful if you please sanction me an advance of ₹ 50,000 against my salary for my daughter's wedding to be held next month.

In consideration of the company granting me the advance, I hereby undertake to repay the advance in 10 monthly installments of ₹ 5,000 each.

I also hereby authorize the company to deduct the monthly installment from my July 2013 salary payable on 1 August 2013.

In the event I leave the employment of the company for any reason whatsoever before the full repayment of the advance, I hereby authorize the company to settle the unpaid amount from my retirement benefit dues.

Thanking you,

Rameshwar Singh

Email Signature Line

4. EMPLOYMENT VERIFICATION LETTER

An Employment Verification Letter is an official document printed on the Company's Letterhead given to its employee.

It is an assurance letter giving the details of employee's income and tenure of employment. Remember the following points:

- It is a formal business communication
- It should be short and to the point
- Confirm the employee's status in the company
- Give precise information about his income

Sample:

Company Letterhead

Date

Manager (Finance)
Westend Finance Corporation
22, Park Street
Kolkata – 700 017

Dear Sir,

This is to certify that Ms Arpita Mitra is a permanent employee of the Westland Finance Corporation working as Deputy Manager (Administration). She has joined in 1997 and is due to retire after attaining the age of 60 in 2025. Her date of birth is 1 August 1965.

She is associated with administrative work and fulfills her duties efficiently and effectively.

Her gross salary per month is ₹ 50,000.

If you require any further information/clarification, please let me know.

Yours faithfully,

Signature

R.S. Sundaram
Manager (Treasury)

5. RECOMMENDATION LETTER FROM EMPLOYER

Company Letterhead

Date

Personnel Manager
Colour Schemes Limited

7, Hungerford Street
Kolkata – 700 017

Dear Sir,

Nilesh Shah has been working with us as Administrative Officer for the last four years. He is responsible for day-to-day administrative work, supervision of the juniors, scheduling meeting and appointments and takes care of the in-house magazine.

His communication skills are outstanding and he performs his duties in a very organized way. He has always ensured that the duties entrusted to him are well done and always meets the deadline without compromising on quality. He is well respected by his colleagues and his juniors are inspired by his motivation. His teamwork is excellent. He is continuously looking for new challenges and has got a positive attitude towards his goals.

He is an asset to our company.

If you need any further information please contact me directly without any hesitation.

Yours faithfully,

Signature

General Manager (Admn)

6. RESIGNATION LETTERS

Resignation letters should be:

- Brief
- Focused
- To the point
- Thankful towards the present employer

Sample:

Sender's Address Line
Date

Mr Raj Kumar Singh
Director (Admn)
Wise Software Company

22, Salt Lake
Kolkata – 700 091

Dear Sir,

After five years of successful association with the company, I am now ready to move on to a more challenging position. It is with a mixture of happiness and regret that I tender my resignation from the services of the company with effect from 1 July 2013.

Thank you for the opportunities for professional and personal development that you have provided me during the last five years. I have gained a great deal of experience which has helped me immensely to grow professionally.

I wish the company all the success in the future.

Yours faithfully,

Signature

Niladri Shah
Manager (Admn)

7. ACCEPTANCE OF RESIGNATION

Sample:

Company Letterhead

Date

Mr Niladri Shah
Manager (Admn)
Wise Software Company

Dear Sir,

We are in receipt of your letter dated 29 May 2013 tendering your resignation from the services of the Wise Software Company with effect from 1 July 2013.

With deep regret we accept your resignation. You have been a true asset of this company and we appreciate your initiative, drive and accomplishment.

We have informed the Accounts Department accordingly and all your dues will be settled before your last working day.

On behalf of the organization we wish you the very best in your future endeavours.

Yours faithfully,

Signature

Raj Kumar Singh
General Manager (Admn)

8. ACCEPTANCE TO A BUSINESS SEMINAR

Sample:

Company Letterhead

Date

Mr P.K. Singh
General Manager (HRD)
National Finance Corporation
67, Havelock Road
Kolkata – 700 033

Dear Sir,

Thank you for your letter dated 2 June 2013, inviting me to speak at the seminar on 'The Millenium Report on the Annual Budget' to be held on 29 June 2013.

I accept with pleasure and look forward to attending the seminar as a speaker. Participation in a seminar like this will give me an opportunity to share my ideas as well as listen to the views of other eminent speakers.

As I will be flying in from Delhi, I would request you to please arrange for a pickup from the airport and overnight accommodation on 29 June 2013.

Wish you every success for the seminar.

Warm regards,

Signature

Vimal Bahri
Chief Finance Officer

To: premkunder.singh@nfcindia.com
Subject: Acceptance to Seminar

Dear Sir,

Thank you for your letter dated 2 June 2013, inviting me to speak at the seminar on 'The Millenium Report on the Annual Budget' to be held on 29 June 2013.

I accept with pleasure and look forward to attending the seminar as a speaker. Participation in a seminar like this will give me an opportunity to share my ideas as well as listen to the views of other eminent speakers.

As I will be flying in from Delhi, I would request you to please arrange for a pickup from the airport and overnight accommodation on 29 June 2013.

Wish you every success for the seminar.

Warm regards,

Vimal Bahri

Email Signature Line

9. WARNING LETTERS

Warning letters are given to employees for various reasons such as – unsatisfactory performance, misconduct, insubordination, among others. A warning letter should be:

- Specific
- Mention the facts correctly
- Be strict

Sample 1:

Company Letterhead

Date

Mr Rajiv Patel
Finance Executive
City Transport Corporation
29, Jhowtala Road
Kolkata – 700 019

Dear Sir,

It has come to our notice that your performance for the last two months has been very unsatisfactory. The information given in your reports is mostly inaccurate or missing. You have been warned in the past, but you have failed to take steps to improve your situation. We offered several alternatives about the possible solution but you have failed to act on them and your performance continues to suffer.

This letter is a warning for your unsatisfactory performance over the past two months. The management and your seniors have been closely evaluating your performance and it is evident that you have been unable to meet the targets allotted to you. The projects entrusted to you are still incomplete even after the extended deadline and this has indirectly cost substantial loss to the company. It is in the best interest of the company that you decide and give a proper explanation for the incomplete targets. Your professional conduct with respect to some of your junior colleagues has also been found to be rude and difficult. Please be advised that failure in your performance can no longer be tolerated and will be subject to strict disciplinary action and can even lead to the termination of your employment with us.

Yours faithfully,

Signature

Manager (Operations)

Sample 2:

Company Letterhead

Date

Mr Rameshwar Yadav
Deputy Manager (Supplies)
City Transport Corporation
29, Jhowtala Road
Kolkata – 700 018

Dear Sir,

We bring to your attention that management has received several reports about your misconduct with other staff members. You have also been using office stationery for your personal use.

It has been reported that you have a domineering attitude towards your juniors and also use abusive language in the office. We consider this to be a serious breach of conduct and take it as an act of threatening your coworkers.

We warn you of harsher alternatives if you fail to improve your behaviour with the staff with immediate effect.

We hope that this letter will act as warning in advance to avoid complications in future. If you would like to discuss your grievances please contact General Manager (Supplies).

Yours faithfully,

Signature

Dipak Singh
(Director Supplies)

10. TERMINATION LETTERS

The issue of termination is an unpleasant duty of the management. It is used as a last resort after counselling and guidance has had no effect on the employee. In case a company is downsizing and employees have to be laid off, the letter must be drafted with extreme care and must be sensitive and accommodating as it is the most unpleasant thing that an employee can face. A termination letter must be:

- Brief and factual
- Polite
- Explain the reason for termination
- Be fair and compassionate
- Detail action according to legal procedure

a. Termination Letter due to Poor Performance

Sample:

Company Letterhead

Date

Mr Pritam Paul
Deputy Manager (Admn)
Western Telecom Limited
24, Backbay Reclamation
Mumbai – 400 020

Dear Sir,

Please refer to our earlier letters and counselling by the Human Resources Department to improve your performance. A review of our records shows that no improvement has taken place in your work. It continues to be substandard and your attitude towards your job has been negative. All our efforts for your betterment proved to be futile. Your negligent attitude threatens the productivity and morale of your co-workers.

Hence, we regret to inform you that your services are no longer required with effect from 13 June 2013.

We are sorry that this step had to be taken but under the circumstances, we are left with no other alternative. Please contact the Finance Department for an early settlement of your dues.

Yours faithfully

Signature

Shyam Kothari
General Manager (HRD)

b. Termination Letter due to Downsizing of the Company

Sample:

Company Letterhead

Date

Mr Rishi Niyogi
Technical Officer
Research and Development Division
Western Telecom Limited
24, Backbay Reclamation
Mumbai – 400 022

Dear Sir,

We regret to inform you that as a result of the merger of our company with Cable Company Limited we have to close down our Research and Development Division and thereby eliminate all the positions in that division. Your position has been included in that. We are sorry that this move has caused so many loyal and valuable employees to leave us.

For some years now we have been going through declining sales due to tough competition in the market. As per the task force recommendation, this downsizing is related to the financial crunch.

This merger was absolutely necessary for our survival and please bear in mind that this is no reflection on your performance. In fact, you have been highly regarded as one of our most productive employees and we appreciate your valuable contributions over the years.

We sympathize and understand the problem of unemployment this will create for you and your family and our Human Resource Department will try their best to assist you with your job search. Given your qualifications and proven abilities, I am confident that you will be able to find another position in the near future. If you want, I could even write a recommendation letter for you.

You will be governed by the company's rules in force with regard to compensation. Please contact the Finance Department for your early settlement.

Meanwhile, please accept our best wishes for future success.

Yours faithfully,

Signature

Shyam Sundar Kothari
Director (Administration)

11. FAREWELL LETTERS TO COLLEAGUES

Writing a farewell letter and then attaching it in a single email to all the addresses in your work email is the best way to bid adieu to all your colleagues and clients and ensures that everyone knows you are leaving a particular organization. This type of letter usually requires only the sender's address and is best sent as an email rather than an attachment or a hard copy. Farewell letters can also be for a sabbatical, or a long personal or medical leave. These should include details of who would be taking on your role while you are away.

Sample 1:

To: all@belltimberindia.com
Subject: Last Day in Office

Dear Friends,

After working for a decade in the Bell Timber Company, I am moving to a new challenging position in another business organization next week. Tomorrow is my last day and I cannot leave without bidding you farewell.

During my association with the company, I have gained valuable experience and without your support and encouragement I would not have grown professionally. I shall always cherish this period in my life. I have always shared a special bonding with all of you. I will all of you and my satisfying stint here.

Please keep in touch by email or on phone. My personal email address and phone numbers are abc@gmail.com.

I wish all of you the very best in both your professional and personal lives.

Yours sincerely,

Mohit Verma

Email Signature Line

Sample 2:

To: all@belltimberindia.com
Subject: Relocation to another City

Dear Friends,

I am writing this letter to inform you that I am leaving the Bell Timber Company as I am relocating to Delhi for personal reasons. Tomorrow is my last working day.

I would like thank all my colleagues for the wonderful time I have had working over here during the last seven years and I will miss all that this place represents. Even though I am moving to a new city and in a different direction, I will always cherish the memories of this place. I will always be grateful for the support and encouragement that has helped me to go forward in life.

I hope we keep in touch in future. My contact details are as before and I welcome your visits when you are in Delhi.

Wish you all the best for your future.

Yours sincerely,

Raj Mohan

Email Signature Line

Farewell Letter for Maternity Leave

To: all@belltimberindia.com
Subject: Maternity Leave

Dear Friends,

As you all know my due date (29 October) is fast approaching and I'm about to get admitted into the hospital any day now. Before I go on maternity leave, I would just like to thank everyone for the support and understanding you have given me the past few months. I do appreciate all of your well wishes.

As for the department files and projects I handle, please forward any concerns to Megha Tripathi as she will be handling my mails and work while I am away. I will have limited access to my email from the first week of December but do call me in case of an emergency.

I wish to see you all at our baby's naming ceremony. It will be wonderful if you join me and my family to give your blessings to our little one. I will write to you with details the date and venue closer to the time.

Warm regards

Kajal Verma

Email Signature Line

12. REQUEST LETTERS

Request letters are of various kinds and can be related to promotions, interviews, reference and recommendation and special information among other things. A request letter within the same organization can be typed on the company letterhead or as an email and requires no additional sender's address line. Request letters should be:

- Polite and courteous
- Specific
- Reasonable
- Confident and persuasive

a. Request for a Promotion

Sample:

Mr Murli Joshi
General Manager (Marketing)
Sun Oil Mill Limited
15, Taratalla Road
Kolkata – 700 077

Dear Sir,

It has been a real learning experience working for the marketing projects. I have been a part of this team for last four years. You have appreciated my work and mentioned it in my last appraisal report and I was also awarded the best employee of the company in the year 2010.

However, I think that the time has come for me to do something more meaningful and important so that I can utilize the knowledge and experience I have gathered under your guidance and leadership. A promotion at a managerial level at this stage will be a great incentive and it will motivate me to produce better work. I can implement lot of ideas with more responsibilities and authorities.

I assure you of my continued dedication and sincere efforts towards my job and hope that I will get an opportunity to serve the company better.

I understand that you have a very busy schedule. I will thus be delighted to meet with you at any time you please to discuss my request.

Yours faithfully,

Signature

Vimal Rawat
Deputy Manager (Sales)

b. Request Letter for Recommendation

Sample:

Mr Murli Joshi
General Manager (Marketing)
Sun Oil Mill Limited
15, Taratalla Road
Kolkata – 700 077

Dear Sir,

I have been associated with this organization for the last 10 years. I have worked under your leadership and guidance for a considerable time. I have been offered a challenging post as Zonal Manager (Marketing) in one of the leading companies dealing with consumer products. I would be grateful if you could please give me a reference letter.

You are a well-known person in the industry and a recommendation letter from you giving an overall assessment of my capabilities will help me to a great extent with my potential employers.

My final interview is next week and if everything works out, I would be required to submit the recommendation letter with my certificates and other papers.

I would also like to take this opportunity to thank you for all the assistance and motivation over the years.

Best regards,

Signature

Vimal Rawat
Deputy Manager (Sales)

c. Request Letter for Information

Sample:

Company Letterhead

Date

Mr Naresh Kumar Jha
Reliable Construction Company
19, Chowringhee Road
Kolkata – 700 016

Dear Sir,

Further to our telephonic discussion, could you please send us copies of the Annual Reports of your company over the last two years.

As I mentioned during our discussion, in addition to the overall financial conditions of your company and its future prospects, we are particularly interested in the performance of your construction projects. It would be helpful if you could please send us additional reports and information regarding your new venture.

Thanking you for your assistance.

Yours faithfully,

Signature

Manab Roy
Manager (Projects)

13. BUSINESS MEMORANDUM

Business memoranda are inter-office correspondence sent between employees, to communicate ideas, convey decisions and to make announcements. They are less informal than business letters. These letters should include all important aspects of the topics they are related to. The format should contain:

- Header
- Names of the addressees where relevant
- Date
- Subject

Sample:

From: Director (Administration)

To: All Divisional Chiefs

Dated 13 June 2013

Subject: Change of name of Insurance Division

With immediate effect, the Insurance Division of the company is now divided into two divisions under the following names:

Insurance Solution will take care of insurance-related matters
Medical Health Product will be responsible for the pharmaceutical products.

We are making this change to facilitate administrative control. The separation of the division will also accelerate growth which is a key factor to success.

Please incorporate the new names immediately for internal and corporate communication.

If you have any suggestion or need any clarification, please contact the undersigned.

Signature

Director (Administration)

To: karanvir.vohra@maprohealthindia.com; rajat.joshi@ maprohealthindia.com; puneet.agarwal@ maprohealthindia. com; mahua.rakesh@ maprohealthindia.com; megha.arora@ maprohealthindia.com; swati.karlekar@ maprohealthindia.com
Subject: Change of name of Insurance Division

With immediate effect, the Insurance Division of the company is divided into two divisions under the following names:

Insurance Solution will take care of insurance-related matters.
Medical Health Product will be responsible for the pharmaceutical products.

We are making this change to facilitate administrative control. The separation of the division will also accelerate growth which is a key factor to success.

Please incorporate the new names immediately for internal and corporate communication.

If you have any suggestion or need any clarification, please contact the undersigned.

Director (Administration)

Email Signature Line

14. COMPANY BONUS LETTER

Sample:

Company Letterhead

Date

All Employees
New Horizon Industry
7, Ballygunge Place
Kolkata – 700 019

Annual Bonus

The management takes pleasure in announcing that an Annual Bonus of ₹ 25,000 will be paid to all employees with the salary for the month of August payable on 1 September 2013. The Bonus is a reflection of the management's appreciation of the employees' sincere work throughout the year.

As the company's financial condition continues to improve, the management will try to provide bonus to its employees every year. The aim is to create a situation where the company prospers and the employees' hard work and support are rewarded properly.

If you have any questions, please contact the Personnel Department.

We wish you all the best for the festive season.

Signature

Director (Administration)

15. JOB TRANSFER LETTERS

Transfer letters are official internal letters issued to the employees asking them to work in a different project or branch.

It might be with a promotion or at the same level. This letter is governed by the clauses of the employee offer letter. Transfer letters should:

- Be short and concise
- Provide clear information about the post, the joining date and associated information
- Give advance notice to the employee to organize his or her affairs
- Assure him of the company's support and assistance in his new role in a new place

a. Job Transfer (From the Company)

Sample:

Company Letterhead

Date

Mr Abhishek Patnaik
Deputy Manager (Services)
Star Computers Limited
Electronic City
Salt Lake
Kolkata – 700 091

Dear Sir,

We have pleasure in informing you that you will be transferred to our Bangalore Zonal Office which will give you different responsibilities. This is a part of our reorganization programme so that we can maximize the potential of our employees. Considering your excellent track record, the management has decided to entrust you with a more challenging job. You will be designated as Manager (Marketing) and will report to the Marketing Head in Bangalore on 1 July 2013. Your compensation will be according to your new grade. We assure you that your seniors will be with you in case you need some help on your new profile. Please see me at my office anytime today for us to discuss some important matters.

I hope that you will excel in your new position. We will always be here to assist you. Should you have concerns or any questions regarding this matter please contact us or any of the managers. I am looking forward to seeing you working in the new department.

Wishing you all the best in your future endeavours.

Yours faithfully,

Signature

Nalin Shah
General Manager (HRD)

b. Job Transfer (Request from an Employee)

Sample:

Company Letterhead

Date

Mr Nalin Shah
General Manager (HRD)
Star Computers Limited
Electronic City
Salt Lake
Kolkata – 700 091

Dear Sir,

I have been working in the Customer Services Department for the last six years. Over the years, I have gathered new skills and grown professionally. I have served the company with sincerity and hard work which went beyond scheduled hours. The company has appreciated my accomplishment with awards and certificates.

I feel that the time is right for me to acquire new skills and experience. Our company plans to bolster its presence in Delhi by opening a new factory in Faridabad which is going to be functional by 2013. The new project is expected to receive all the clearances from Government by end 2013 and the construction work will start in 2012.

I would like to be associated with this project where my skill and experience can be utilized to the maximum. The additional responsibility will broaden my horizon and will help me to move my career forward in the company.

Thank you for your consideration. We can meet at your convenience and discuss the matter in further detail.

Yours faithfully,

Signature

Abhishek Patnaik
Deputy Manager (Customer Services)

16. REJECTION LETTERS BY EMPLOYERS

Job rejection letters by potential employers should be very clear and convey the message without a shadow of doubt so that the addressee gets the point immediately. The letter should be:

- Polite and courteous
- Brief
- To the point

Sample:

Company Letterhead

Date

Mr Abhirup Bedi
179, Jhowtala Road
Kolkata – 700 017

Dear Sir,

Thank you for your interest in the Project Engineer's position advertised in the paper recently. We enjoyed meeting you.

Selecting a final candidate was difficult. However, we have selected another candidate who is well qualified and best meets our current needs. We are sorry to inform you that you are not selected for this job. Our choice in no way reflects upon your excellent skills and abilities.

We sincerely wish you the best of luck in your job search and thanks once again for your interest in our organization.

Yours faithfully,

Signature

Mr Satyajit Pakrashi
Director (HR)

17. WELCOME LETTERS

These letters should be friendly and introduce the new member to the organization and inform about orientation programs if any. There should be a brief history of the company along with a congratulatory note. Letters to welcome new clients aboard should reiterate the history and quality of services associated with the company and mention incentives if any.

a. Welcome Letter to a New Employee

Sample:

Company Letterhead

Date

Mr Sarat Mehta
24, Andheri West
Mumbai – 400 072

Dear Mr Mehta,

It is with great pleasure we welcome you to Modern Software Company. We are delighted you are joining us as Project Engineer on 1 August 2013.

This is to inform you that the new employees orientation meet will be on 3 August 2013. You will meet the Human Resources Department to discuss your service integration into our organization and to learn about employment related issues. You will also be introduced to your colleagues who will explain the overall work of the department.

We have a proud heritage of service to the IT Industry and we welcome deserving people like you to take initiative to assist us to improve our company's mission. We look forward working with you.

If you have any specific questions, please contact me or the HR Department. We will do our best to help you to settle down in your new position.

Thanks for joining us and we wish you all the best in your new position.

Yours sincerely,

Signature

Raghav Taneja
Director (Projects)

To: sarat.mehta@modernsoftwareindia.com
Subject: Welcome

Dear Mr Mehta,

It is with great pleasure we welcome you to Modern Software Company. We are delighted you are joining us as Project Engineer on 1 August 2013.

This is to inform you that the new employees orientation meet will be on 3 August 2013. You will meet the Human Resources Department to discuss your service integration into our organization and to learn about employment-related issues. You will also be introduced to your colleagues who will explain the overall work of the department.

We have a proud heritage of service to the IT Industry and we welcome deserving people like you to take initiative to assist us to improve our company's mission. We look forward working with you.

If you have any specific questions, please contact me or the HR Department. We will do our best to help you to settle down in your new position.

Thanks for joining us and we wish you all the best in your new position.

Yours sincerely,

Raghav Taneja

Email Signature Line

b. Welcome Letter to a New Client

Sample:

Company Letterhead

Date

Mr Mayur Binani
General Manager (Corporate Development)
Surya Cables Limited
43, Prince Anwar Shah Road
Kolkata – 700 031

Dear Sir,

We are delighted that you have chosen Modern Software Limited to cater to your needs. It is our aim to meet your expectations.

Please find enclosed a brochure and a welcome pack with your code number which should be used in all future correspondence. As a part of our introduction to new clients, you are entitled to a 10% discount on your first order.

We will provide you with our complete line of products and services at a competitive price. Our commitment to excellence will become evident as you deal with our professional team. We are a customer-oriented company and will provide the best service to our valued customers. We look forward to our continued mutually satisfactory business relationship with your company.

If you need any further information or clarification, please contact us and we will provide you all possible assistance.

Yours faithfully,

Signature

Rishav Puri
General Manager (Projects)

18. COLLECTION LETTERS

The purpose of writing a collection letter is to persuade someone to make payment of the outstanding dues. It should contain:

- The reason behind the letter
- Time frame of payment
- Suggest a solution

a. Collection Letter (Demanding Payment)

Sample 1:

Company Letterhead

Date

Mr Raman Nair
Super Bike Company Limited
23, R.K. Puram
New Delhi – 110 022

Dear Sir,

We find from our records that the invoice for the shipment of spare parts dated 15 March 2013 has been outstanding for more than three months. We sent you a reminder last month pointing out the non-payment of our bill. Your letter dated 20 May along with a cheque for partial payment indicated a minor cash flow problem and gave a payment schedule to settle the dues.

As of 21 June 2013, we have not received any further payment. You failed to inform us about the delay. Please send the payment immediately or contact us to avoid further collection reminders.

We want to assist you to meet your commitment without causing undue pressure and are ready to discuss a new payment schedule. We have some payment options to suit your present financial crunch. Please contact the undersigned without further delay for an amicable solution of the problem.

Your cooperation in the matter is appreciated.

Yours faithfully,

Signature

Parthiv Rai
Finance Manager

Sample 2:

Company Letterhead

Date

Mr Raman Nair
Super Bike Company Limited
23, R. K. Puram
New Delhi – 110 022

Dear Sir,

We have written to you numerous letters and sent reminders thereafter for non-payment of our bills dated 3 January 2013 and 25 Janaury 2013. We even offered you proposals with easy payment schedules, however, you have not responded to our communication.

We expect payment in full within 10 days. If the payment is not received or you fail to contact us, your account will be turned over to a collection bureau for investigation of the case and if necessary, start legal proceedings.

Your prompt action in this matter will be appreciated.

Yours faithfully,

Signature

Parthiv Rai
Finance Manager

b. Collection Letter (Promising Payment)

Sample:

Company Letterhead

Date

Parthiv Rai
Finance Manager
Eastern Tools Limited
24, B.T. Road
Kolkata – 700 039

Dear Sir,

We are in receipt of your reminder for late payment of your bills. We appreciate your offer for rescheduling the payment arrangement to help us to resolve the financial crisis.

Due to the current financial situation caused by a slowdown in the economy, we have decided to implement a new scheme which will improve our cash flow. We anticipate that within a month normalcy will be restored and we will be in a position to settle all your outstanding dues. In the meantime we enclose a cheque for ₹ 10 lakh in part payment.

We appreciate your patience and flexibility and look forward to our continued business relationship.

Thanking you,

Signature

Raman Nair
Accounts Manager

To: parthiv.rai@easterntoolsindia.com
Subject: Promise of Payment

Dear Sir,

We are in receipt of your reminder for late payment of your bills. We appreciate your offer for rescheduling the payment arrangement to help us to resolve the financial crisis.

Due to the current financial situation caused by a slowdown in the economy, we have decided to implement a new scheme which will improve our cash flow. We anticipate that within a month normalcy will be restored and we will be in a position to settle all your outstanding dues. In the meantime we enclose a cheque for ₹ 10 lakh in part payment.

We appreciate your patience and flexibility and look forward to our continued business relationship.

Thanking you,

Raman Nair

Email Signature Line

19. INVOICE COVERING LETTER

Invoice letters are written while submitting an invoice to a company for the items supplied or services rendered. The letter should be:

- Formal
- Specific about payment clause

Sample:

Company's Letterhead

Date

Mr Naresh Pathak
Manager (Purchase)
Greenlight Electronics Limited
21, Chowringhee Square
Kolkata – 700 001

Dear Sir,

We submit herewith our invoice dated 22 June 2013, for an amount of ₹ 20 lakh for the material supplied to your Taratala factory pursuant to your order dated 1 June 2013. We have offered you 2% discount on your bill. To avail of this offer, payment should be made within a month of submitting the invoice.

Please let us know if you have any question or need any clarification regarding this invoice.

We appreciate the opportunity to do business with you.

Yours faithfully,

Signature

Nil Ratan Patel
Manager (Supplies)

20. FUNDRAISING LETTER

A carefully, targeted, well-written letter is the key factor for Donation/Fund Raising projects. It should not be complicated and explain clearly the cause of the organization. The format is as follows:

- Clearly mention the name and address of the organization
- Address of the donor
- Well explained causes

- Request for donation
- Include a prepaid envelope

Sample 1:

Company Letterhead

Date

Mr Motilal Mehta
124, Ballygunge Circular Road
Kolkata – 700 019

Dear Mr Mehta,

We are approaching you on behalf of Happy Home Mission, which is a charity organization and totally depends on the contributions of generous patrons like yourself. We are committed to improve the lives of slum children. Through our educational scholarships and free lunch programmes, we have been able to make an impact on the lives of these neglected, poverty-stricken children.

In the current financial climate with inflation going sky high, it is becoming increasingly difficult to provide our free services to the community. The purpose of this letter is to request you to consider a donation to a good cause.

Any amount you donate will help us to serve our society better. To make a donation please fill in the pledge card and send it along with your cheque in the prepaid envelope. Your donation will be exempted from taxes.

On behalf of our organization, I thank you for considering a contribution. Please send your donation by 15 July 2013.

Yours sincerely,

Signature

Ramesh Parekh

Secretary

To: motilal.mehta@belltimberindia.com
Subject: Request for Donation

Dear Mr Mehta,

We are approaching you on behalf of Happy Home Mission, which is a charity organization and totally depends on the contributions of generous patrons like yourself. We are committed to improve the lives of slum children. Through our educational scholarships and free lunch programmes, we have been able to make an impact on the lives of these neglected, poverty-stricken children.

In the current financial climate with inflation going sky high, it is becoming increasingly difficult to provide our free services to the community. The purpose of this letter is to request you to consider a donation to a good cause.

Any amount you donate will help us to serve our society better. To make a donation please fill in the pledge card that we have sent you by post and send it along with your cheque in the prepaid envelope (also in the same package). Your donation will be exempted from taxes.

On behalf of our organization, I thank you for considering a contribution. Please send your donation by 15 July 2013.

Yours sincerely,

Ramesh Parekh

Email Signature Line

Sample 2:

Sender's Address Line
Date

Mr Subhash Rao
189, Ballygunge Place
Kolkata – 700 019

Dear Mr Rao,

Our organization, Animal Shelter, houses almost 5,000 homeless, lost, neglected and maltreated animals. We provide free shelter, medical services and run an adoption programme so that they can be settled in good homes.

To be able to continue our mission, we need a quite sizeable fund and Animal Shelter is a non-profit organization. We rely totally on donations from concerned people like you to protect these animals from harsh and inhuman conditions.

We are proud of our accomplishment and like every year, we are hosting our annual fundraising programme this year as well. There will be a dinner where all patrons will be invited to contribute to our organization. We humbly request our donors for all possible financial assistance to keep our organization going. These donations are fully tax-deductible.

We are enclosing the invitation card for the event and earnestly hope that you will be able to attend the dinner.

Thank you in advance for your compassion and support.

Together we can save and cherish these innocent and adorable animals.

Yours sincerely,

Signature

Mrinalini Desai
Managing Member

21. DEMAND PAYMENT LETTER

Generally, these letters are written to claim dues from defaulting clients. This type of letter should:

- Verify the contract related to the transaction
- Mention specifically the breach of contract
- Allow a time frame for payment
- Inform the client about legal action in case of non-payment within the prescribed time limit
- Have a polite yet strict tone

Sample 1:

Company Letterhead

Date

Mr Ranjan Sharma
300, Southern Avenue
Kolkata – 700 029

Dear Sir,

We find from our records that you have an outstanding balance of ₹ 10 lakh lying unpaid for the last six months. Our numerous reminders failed to yield any result. This is your final notice.

We are giving you one month's time to repay the entire outstanding dues. In the event of non-payment within the prescribed time limit we will have no other option but to resort to legal action against you. Interest at the penalty rate of 15% on the amount will continue to accrue.

If you have any question or need any clarification, please get in touch with the undersigned without any further delay.

Your prompt action will be appreciated.

Yours faithfully,

Signature

Swarup Sethia
Manager (Loan Recovery)

Sample 2:

Company Letterhead

Date

Mr Arnab Chand
Manager (Supplies)
Green Cable Company Limited
191, Salt Lake City
Kolkata – 700 091

Dear Sir,

We would like to point out that an amount of ₹ 50 lakh due for payment within 31 March 2013 remains outstanding in spite of numerous written reminders and telephone calls. During the last 3 months we have had several discussions to resolve the matter.

This amount is due against our shipment of goods supplied to you six months back (January 2013). The payment clause of your order clearly states that payment will be made within 60 days of receipt of the goods. Till date you have not shown any inclination to settle the dues. Unless we receive the full payment within 15 days, we will have no other alternative but to exercise our legal rights to recover the payment.

You are also liable to pay an interest charge of 5% on the entire amount from 1 April 2013 till the date of payment.

Your immediate action is required.

Yours faithfully,

Signature

Mohan Thapa
Manager (Finance)

22. CIRCULARS/NOTICES

Circular letters are issued to a number of people to communicate the same information. It is a formal way to providing business news. Internal circulars are meant for employees only and deals with organizational affairs, whereas external circulars are sent to customers and clients. They usually convey information about change of address, launch of a new product, service, or announce a discount. Circulars never convey any confidential matter. All circulars should keep in mind the following points:

- The purpose should be clear
- The language should be simple and precise
- The basic idea must be convincing and interesting

a. Change of Address

Sample:

Company Letterhead

Date

To All Customers,

Due to the expansion of our business, it has became necessary for the company to shift to larger premises to render better services to our customers. Our new premises are spacious and easily accessible by rail and road. We have adequate parking spaces for all our clients. You will have no difficulty in visiting our office in the future.

Our Old address: 34, Strand Road
Kolkata – 700 001

Our New Address: 225, N.S. Road
Kolkata – 700 001

Our existing telephone numbers remain unchanged.

Any inconvenience caused to our valued customers is regretted.

We take this opportunity to convey our thanks for your support and assure you of our sincere efforts to serve you better in future.

Signature

General Manager (Admn)

b. Holiday Notices

Sample:

Company Letterhead

Date

To All Employees,

This is to inform you that 23 August 2013 has been declared a holiday due to state elections. All the establishments of the Bell Timber Company will remain closed on that day.

Regards,

Signature

Managing Director

To: all@belltimberindia.com
Subject: Public Holiday

To All Employees,

This is to inform you that 23 August 2013 has been declared a holiday due to state elections. All the establishments of the Bell Timber Company will remain closed on that day.

Regards,

Managing Director

Email Signature Line

23. CONTRACT LETTER FOR AUDIT

All business concerns are required to get their accounts audited by certified auditors as per the statutory law of the land. The following is a sample contract letter of engagement for auditors.

Sample:

Company Letterhead

Date

Messrs Wilson & Smith
Chartered Accountants
332, Bhikaji Kama Place
New Delhi – 110066

Dear Sirs,

We have pleasure in appointing you to act as our Auditor for the year 2010–11 on the following terms and conditions:

1) You will be responsible under the prevailing Rules and Regulations for preparing the annual accounts including all the financial transactions and to ensure that the company has complied with the all the provisions of the guidelines issued by the Government of India.
2) Your managers would cooperate with us to facilitate the audit work.
3) Our company has a statutory requirement to file the Accounts Report for the financial year ending 31 March 2013 by 30 April 2013. The following matters should be considered before the final submission.
   a) Whether the company's balance sheet conforms to the books of accounts.
   b) Whether the books of accounts and other financial records have been properly maintained.
   c) Whether all the information and explanation pertaining to the report are available.
   d) Whether non-compliance, if any, is justified under the circumstances.
4) The audit will be conducted according to the Standard Auditing Guidelines issued by the Government of India and comply with the existing rules.
5) To safeguard the interest of our company and to prevent misappropriation of funds or any other non-compliance with law, we would expect you to detect any such act if it exists.

In consideration of the performance of the provisions of this contract to audit accounts, the company shall pay the Auditors a sum of ₹ 20 lakh as the fees and expenses related to the audit.

Please confirm in writing your approval of the terms and conditions mentioned above within 10 days from the date of this letter.

Please let us know if you need any further information or clarification.

Thanking you,

Signature

Finance Director

24. PERFORMANCE EVALUATION LETTER

Performance appraisal is meant to assess and evaluate an employee's overall performance for the year. It analyses the capabilities and shortfalls of the employees. It basically depends on the employees work quality, output, attitude and behaviour. The evaluation letter format should be:

- Just and fair
- Consistent
- Recognition of positive results
- Suggest measures to improve weak areas
- Include performance-related ratings

a. Good Performance

Sample:

Company Letterhead

Date

Mr Manoj Sahai
Manager (Supplies)
Edible Oil Mills Limited
Gardenreach
Kolkata – 700 027

Dear Sir,

We have reviewed your performance for the year 2010–11 and have pleasure to inform you that your output has been excellent. Your dedication and commitment is evident in all spheres of your job. It was consistent and exceeds expectation. Your positive attitude towards your job has motivated your team to achieve a higher target which has helped the company's productivity.

We have given you a rating of 6 which would make you eligible for further promotion immediately. A separate letter giving all the details of your designation and new grade will be issued shortly.

We are looking forward to your excellent performance in the future.

Yours faithfully,

Signature

Raghav Mohan

General Manager (HR)

To: manoj.sahai@zindaoilindia.com
Subject: Appraisal

Dear Sir,

We have reviewed your performance for the year 2010–11 and have pleasure to inform you that your output has been excellent. Your dedication and commitment is evident in all spheres of your job. It was consistent and exceeds expectation. Your positive attitude towards your job has motivated your team to achieve a higher target which has helped the company's productivity.

We have given you a rating of 6 which would make you eligible for further promotion immediately. A separate letter giving all the details of your designation and new grade will be issued shortly.

We are looking forward to your excellent performance in the future.

Yours faithfully,

Raghav Mohan

Email Signature Line

b. Below-Average Performance

Sample:

Company Letterhead

Date

Mr Samir Bhandari
Deputy Manager (Purchase)
Westend Industries Limited
175, Taratalla Road
Kolkata – 700 029

Dear Sir,

We have just reviewed your performance for the 2010–11 and regret to inform you that it is below the standard the company has set for its employees.

You had not made any effort to utilize the resources at your disposal to implement your projects. In this regard, I would specifically mention that the project reports prepared by you for the upcoming mining projects are superficial and lack focus. As a result it did not serve any purpose and has no use for the company.

As a corrective measure we are suggesting that you join the three-month training programme on 'Work Strategy'. It will take care of your shortfalls and help you to produce better results in future.

In case you are having any problems with your present role, please let me know and I will discuss the matter with you.

Yours faithfully,

Signature

Raman Shobhraj
Director (Purchase)

25. MARKETING LETTER TO PROMOTE AN EVENT

The objective of a marketing letter is to generate interest about the event among the readers. It should be addressed to the specific audience who is related to the event either as participants or contributors. To make the event a success the readers should be motivated to attend it. It is an effective way to start the company's marketing campaign. The letter should mention:

- Date and venue of the event
- Reason behind the event
- Summary of the programme

Sample:

Company's Letterhead

Date

Vice President (Power)
Orient Solar Energy Limited
33, Budge Budge Trunk Road
Kolkata – 700 027

Dear Sir,

We have pleasure in announcing that our annual event on environmental issues will be held on 22 August 2013 at Brigade Parade Ground from 9 a.m. to 8 p.m. The event is called 'Thought for Tomorrow'. There will be an exhibition and seminars to create awareness amongst the public about the importance of a clean environment and to realize the serious effects of air pollution, deforestation, global warming and other related topics.

Your organization paved the way by generating power without polluting the environment and you remain among the frontrunners in this enterprise. We are writing to invite you to participate in the event. Your expertise and guidelines will help us in our goal to project the need to use natural resources for our daily requirement. We have emphasized on the importance of organic farming and are planning to show the harmful side effects of pesticides on food grains through visual modes. With your active participation we will try to appeal to the public for a safer tomorrow devoid of pollution.

We are looking forward to welcoming you to an exciting and successful event.

If you would like any further information or clarification, please contact the undersigned without any hesitation.

Thanks for your support.

Yours faithfully,

Signature

Raman Gomes
General Manager (Projects)

To: vivan.sundar@orientsolarindia.com
Subject: Environement Exhibition

Dear Sir,

We have pleasure in announcing that our annual event on environmental issues will be held on 22 August 2013 at Brigade Parade Ground from 9 a.m. to 8 p.m. The event is called 'Thought for Tomorrow'. There will be an exhibition and seminars to create awareness amongst the public about the importance of a clean environment and to realize the serious effects of air pollution, deforestation, global warming and other related topics.

Your organization paved the way by generating power without polluting the environment and you remain among the frontrunners in this enterprise. We are writing to invite you to participate in the event. Your expertise and guidelines will help us in our goal to project the need to use natural resources for our daily requirement. We have emphasized on the importance of organic farming and are planning to show the harmful side effects of pesticides on food grains through visual modes. With your active participation we will try to appeal to the public for a safer tomorrow devoid of pollution.

We are looking forward to welcoming you to an exciting and successful event.

If you would like any further information or clarification, please contact the undersigned without any hesitation.

Thanks for your support.

Yours faithfully,

Raman Gomes

Email Signature Line

26. SALES LETTER TO PROMOTE A PRODUCT

A business sales letter is written to attract the attention of the potential customers. The product should be presented in such a way so that it looks better than that of the competitors and is available at a lesser cost. The tone of the letter should be informal and friendly. The letter should contain:

- A short eye-catching heading
- Highlights of the special features and benefits
- Cost-to-value ratio
- Special offers

Sample:

Company Letterhead

Date

Manager (Admn)
Oriental Electronics Limited
179, Diamond Harbour Road
Kolkata – 700 027

Dear Sir,

Super Space-Saving Modular Office Furniture is Now Here!

Excel Interiors is launching a new line of Modular Office Furniture to cater to your special requirement. As a full service provider, we design and refurbish your whole office with special attention to the reception area and conference rooms. They are designed and made to suit your specifications and installed by us at no extra cost. As you are one of our most valued customers, we are offering a discount of 20% on this new line of furniture. This offer is valid till end of August 2013.

This new product is termite-resistant and made with imported Malayasian rose wood. The furniture is long-lasting and costs much less than teak wood. Our product is also guaranteed for 3 years and we offer the best price in the market.

We have enclosed a detailed brochure outlining the products' specifications and we would request you to read it. If you decide that our product meets with your requirements, please contact us at your earliest to avail of our best offer.

Yours faithfully,

Signature

Shivraj Nair
Manager (Supplies)

27. BUSINESS PROPOSAL LETTER

It is a covering letter giving a brief description of the proposal. The important features that make it different from others is highlighted. The aim of this letter is to gain more business for the company. The format should contain:

- Remedies to improve the present situation
- Feasibility of the proposal
- Past reference – completion of successful projects
- Definite time frame

Sample:

Company Letterhead

Date

Administrative Manager
City Transport Corporation
23, Karl Marx Sarani
Kolkata – 700 023

Dear Sir,

This has reference to the series of discussions we had had regarding the productivity of your company. We submit herewith our business proposal specially formulated to cater to your requirements.

We are going to put your entire operating system under review and find out the shortcomings. The proposal suggests remedies to correct the situation. Modern technology will be implemented to replace the traditional method of operation which will reduce cost and save manpower. The aim is to move towards a paperless office.

The enclosed proposal gives a broad outline of the process. We have also mentioned our similar successful projects for your detailed study and consideration.

If you need any further information or clarification, please contact us.

Once you approve our proposal we will finalize all other details.

Best regards,

Signature

Man Mohan Shah
Operating Manager

Application Letters

This type of letter should deal with all aspects of job application. It is an extremely important kind of letter that could determine your future prospects as well as details of your employment in a new organization. From how you present yourself in a cover letter while applying for a job to negotiating an offer, application letters should stress on clarity, creativity and composition.

Every application letter must clearly state details of education, past work experience and numbers and figures that might have been agreed upon verbally.

Cover letters should be creative and display your personality as well as appropriateness for a particular job. This kind of a letter should market the candidate in a manner that will immediately catch the attention of a prospective employer.

The language used in application letters should be impeccable and the letter should be composed with thought. It should state all the relevant points and avoid any kind of repetition or unnecessary details.

1. COVER LETTER

Resumes should be sent with a cover letter specifying the post applied for and it is based on the information provided in the resume. This is an all-important letter and sometimes even determines whether your resume will get read or not. It should be a marketing letter which should be targeted towards the organization in question. The letter should also reflect your attitude, personality, motivation and communication skills. At the same time, it should be brief and to the point and it should not repeat information already laid out in your resume. All cover letters should include the following points:

- There should be a heading outlining which position your are applying for
- If it is an unsolicited application, make sure that you mention which department you want to work in and in what kind of a position (full-time, contract, part-time, or internship)
- Put in brief details/highlights of your educational background and work experience relevant for the application.

a. Cover Letter for an Advertised Position

Sample:

Date
Sender's Address Line

General Manager (HRD)
Greenfield Electronics Company Limited
25, Aruna Asaf Ali Marg
New Delhi – 110 067

Application for the Post of Public Relations Officer

Dear Sir,

This has reference to your advertisement in the *Times of India* dated 5 November 2013, for the post of Public Relations Officer in your concern.

I am keen to work for a reputed organization like yours where there are opportunities to learn and enrich one's experience. You have mentioned in your advertisement that you are looking for a motivated and goal-oriented individual. I would like to present myself as a suitable candidate.

I have done a two-year Public Relations Diploma course which has provided me with the necessary communication skills to deal with the media as well as manage the communications of your esteemed company.

My work experience in the communications, media and social media divisions of an MNC bank has given me sound knowledge to deal with customers and the general public.

The enclosed resume is a brief summary of my qualifications, experience and other job-related information.

I look forward to an interview with you at your convenience.

Warm regards,

Signature

Rajan Ranganath

b. Unsolicited Cover Letter

This particular letter is written to potential employers for job opportunities without any intimation about any openings. The letter should be brief, specific, informative and should be able to attract the attention of the employer. It is a self-marketing letter written in a confident manner without being aggressive. It should communicate your purpose clearly and completely and mention the kind of position/work you are looking for.

Sample:

Sender's Address Line
Date

The Personnel Manager
Blue Cross Pharmaceutical Company Limited
35, Ballard Estate
Mumbai – 400 012

Dear Sir,

Your organization is the most sought after pharmaceutical company in India. You have recently announced your expansion plan to cater to new clients in eastern India which will open up new job opportunities.

With more than eight years experience in an MNC pharmaceutical company in the East, I have successfully marketed several new products. I am familiar with all aspects of sales and marketing, launching of new products, establishing new contacts and selecting distribution agents.

This region is my stronghold and I would be able to tap into my database to further your business interests here. I would be pleased to provide you with any additional information you may require and look forward to meeting you for an interview at your convenience for further discussion. A copy of my resume is enclosed herewith.

Yours faithfully,

Signature

Subhash Kirkire

To: jobs@bluecrosspharmaindia.com
Subject: Enquiry about Sales Position in the East

Dear Sir,

Your organization is the most sought after pharmaceutical company in India. You have recently announced your expansion plan to cater to new clients in eastern India which will open up new job opportunities.

With more than eight years experience in an MNC pharmaceutical company in the East, I have successfully marketed several new products. I am familiar with all aspects of sales and marketing, launching of new products, establishing new contacts and selecting distribution agents.

This region is my stronghold and I would be able to tap into my database to further your business interests here. I would be pleased to provide you with any additional information you may require and look forward to meeting you for an interview at your convenience for further discussion.

Yours faithfully,

Subhash Kirkire

Email Signature Line

2. ACCEPTANCE LETTER

Acceptance letters are basically written to acknowledge the confirmation of a job offer. It is preferable to accept the offer through formal written communication. The letter should be brief and specific mentioning the following:

- Thanks for the offer
- Acceptance of the terms and conditions
- Joining date

Letters accepting a job offer will be kept on record and will establish a contractual relationship between you and the organization. Thus, it is of extreme importance that these letters should reiterate the agreed terms and conditions and put them down in a form that can be used for future reference in case any dispute arises.

Sample 1:

Sender's Address Line
Date

General Manager (Admin)
Redstone Company Pvt Ltd
66, B.N. Mukherjee Road
Kolkata – 700 001

Dear Sir,

Thank you for the Appointment Letter dated 4 June 2013, offering me the post of Manager (Admn) in your organization. I am pleased to confirm my acceptance for the offer at a salary of ₹ 22,56,000 CTC per annum.

As per our discussion we had during the final interview, I shall be able to report for duty on 1 July 2013. Please let me know if you require any further documentation from my side or need me to come in to complete any other formalities before the joining date.

I would like to thank you once again for giving me this opportunity. I am looking forward to a challenging and fulfilling career with your company.

Yours faithfully,

Signature

Arun Mehta

Sample 2:

Sender's Address Line
Date

General Manager (HR)
Green Valley Constructions Limited
333 Strand Road
Kolkata – 700 001

Dear Sir,

Thank you for your generous offer. I am delighted to accept the post of Project Manager with your concern.

I would like to join your employment on 1 January 2012 as I need some time to complete the unfinished projects before I move out.

Thank you for the wonderful opportunity. I look forward to the new challenges and will put in my best efforts to make a positive contribution towards the company's goals.

The signed copies of the Confidentiality Agreement and Salary Contract are returned herewith.

Yours faithfully,

Signature

Rohit Rao

3. REJECTION LETTER

A Rejection letter should also be clear and precise and also thank the company for the opportunity that was provided. Rejection letters should be written after due consideration of the offer – remuneration, benefits, prerequisites and the ambience of the work place. The letter should be polite and specific reasons for denial of the job is not necessary.

Sample 1:

Sender's Address Line
Date

Mr Satyajit Pakrashi
Director (HR)
Anand Medical Company Limited
35, Taratalla Road
Kolkata – 700 027

Dear Sir,

Thank you very much for offering me the position of Marketing Manager with your company but I must decline the offer. It was a difficult choice to make, but I have accepted a position with another company which is better suited to my experience and qualifications.

I sincerely appreciate your taking the time and effort to interview me and to share information on the opportunities available in your company.

Please accept my sincere regrets and thanks against for your job offer.

Best regards,

Signature

Anurag Roy

Sample 2:

Sender's Address Line
Date

General Manager (HR)
Ace Computers Limited
22, North Kali Temple Road
Kolkata – 700045

Dear Sir,

Thank you very much for your letter dated 9 April 2012, offering me the post of Senior Engineer in your concern.

However after a detailed evaluation of the offer I regret to inform you that I am unable to accept your offer.

Thank you once again for considering me for the position. I wish your company all the success in the future.

Yours faithfully,

Signature

R.K. Singh

To: hr@aceindia.com
Subject: Regarding Job Offer

Dear Sir,

Thank you very much for your letter dated 9 April 2012, offering me the post of Senior Engineer in your concern.

However after a detailed evaluation of the offer I regret to inform you that I am unable to accept your offer.

Thank you once again for considering me for the position. I wish your company all the success in the future.

Yours faithfully,

R.K. Singh

Email Signature Line

4. CLARIFICATION LETTER

A clarification letter should clearly highlight the questions that the potential employee might have and be able to glean all the answers from the addressee before one can write a final acceptance or rejection letter.

It is very important to thoroughly evaluate the job offer before making the right decision. Any doubts regarding benefit and perks should be cleared and additional information and clarifications should be sought before final acceptance.

Sample:

Sender's Address Line
Date

General Manager (HR)
Green Valley Constructions Limited
333 Strand Road
Kolkata – 700 001

Dear Sir,

Thank you very much for your offer letter dated 20 November 2013, for the post of Administrative Manager in your company. Before formally accepting the position I would like to have some additional information and clarification regarding the following benefits and parks.

I would be grateful if you could please send me the details of Medical Insurance benefits for the family.

I would also like to know the exact HRA amount as well as the transport allowance offered by the company.

Once I have clarity on these questions, I will send you my formal acceptance by 15 December 2013.

I look forward to working with you.

Yours faithfully,

Signature

Raman Raheja

Bank and Insurance Letters

Correspondence with banks regarding various aspects of banking requires systematic assessment of the situation before the actual letters are written.

For an effective communication with a bank – letters should be brief, specific and yet it should provide all the important information especially the account number and any prior communication, so that the required clarification and action from the bank's end can be easily facilitated.

Letters should be addressed to the specific department dealing with the relevant matter for speedy redressal.

Letters should be polite and professional even if it is a complaint against the bank. Unnecessary details should be avoided.

Bank and insurance letters should be divided into paragraphs for easy reading. The first paragraph should clearly mention the purpose of the letter. Supporting paragraphs should deal with anticipated action from bank. At the end of the letter, the sender's name, address, account number should be clearly stated.

In case the letter requires additional documents, attach scanned copies to the body of the email after signing and attesting the originals or simply send attested photocopies of the necessary documents to your branch, or relationship manager, or insurance agent. The original documents are usually produced for verification across the table.

INSURANCE LETTERS (CLAIMS):

Insurance letters should be courteous, formal and assertive. Here are the main features for an effective claim letter:

- Clearly specify the type of claim
- Mention the policy and other important reference numbers
- Clearly mention the amount of the claim
- All the relevant documents should be enclosed with the claim
- Claim should be sent within the particular time frame

1. LETTERS OF FINANCE CREDIT

These letters are generally written asking for particular information related to bank accounts and credit cards as well as loan history. The format should be:

- Short and specific
- Furnish required information
- Formal
- Give contact information
- Mention the account number

a. Credit Card Offer Letter

Sample:

Bank Letterhead

Date

Mr Raj Kumar Nair
Manager (Admn)
City Transport Corporation Limited
23, Karl Marx Sarani
Kolkata – 700 023

Dear Sir,

After an extensive market survey, we are pleased to inform you that your company qualifies for our prestigious Gold Corporate Credit Cards package for your employees. We are very selective of the customers to whom we offer credit. This measure helps to keep our bad debt to minimum and permits us to offer competitive rates to our customers.

Please fill up the attached application form and send it to us for further action. You can apply on line or can call us at our toll-free number given in the form.

There is no annual fee and rewards start at 1000 points. You can choose your gift from the enclosed catalogue.

We want you to take advantage of our special deals that are on offer till 30 June 2013.

Welcome to our family and we look forward to a happy association.

Yours faithfully,

Signature

Roop Kumar Trivedi
Customer Service Manager

b. Application for a Credit Card

This is a request letter asking the bank to provide credit card facility to an existing customer. The letter should give adequate information sought by the bank as well as income proof from the employer along with the latest salary statement attested by an authorized manager.

Sample:

Sender's Address Line
Phone Number/Email Address
Account Number
Date

Senior Manager
Customer Services Department
Universal Bank Limited
Ballard Estate Branch
25, Ballard Estate
Mumbai – 400 036

Dear Sir,

I would request you to issue a Visa credit card in my name. I have a savings account with your bank for the last 10 years. I also have fixed deposits of ₹ 15,00,000 in your bank.

As per the terms and conditions for issuing a new credit card, I am enclosing my salary statements duly attested by the authorized representative of the company, two copies of address proof and two copies of self-attested photographs.

Two copies of credit card application forms, duly filled in, are attached herewith.

If you need any further information/clarification please let me know.

Prompt action in this matter would be highly appreciated.

Thanking you,

Signature

Subhnarayan Gupta

To: customercare@universalbankindia.com
Subject: Application for a Credit Card

Name:
Account No:

Dear Sir,

I would request you to issue a Visa credit card in my name. I have a savings account with your bank for the last 10 years. I also have fixed deposits of ₹ 15,00,000 in your bank.

As per the terms and conditions for issuing a new credit card, I am enclosing scanned copies of my salary statements duly attested by the authorized representative of the company, two copies of address proof and two copies of self-attested photographs.

I have sent you the filled credit card application forms by post.

If you need any further information/clarification please let me know.

Prompt action in this matter would be highly appreciated.

Thanking you,

Subhnarayan Gupta

Email Signature Line

c. Cancelling a Credit Card

Sample:

Sender's Address Line
Phone Number/Email Address
Account Number
Date

Roop Kumar Trivedi
Customer Service Manager
Western Bank Limited
1B, Greater Kailash Part II
New Delhi – 110 012

Dear Sir,

I would request you to close my Credit Card (Western Visa) Account with immediate effect. I have enclosed a cheque for the outstanding amount due to the bank. If any other amount is due please inform me and I will pay it without any delay.

Your 10% interest rate seems to be higher than any other bank in the market. Your service has deteriorated over the years and your recent interest hike also makes it difficult for me to continue transactions with your bank.

Thanks for a year of credit and good service in the past.

Yours faithfully,

Signature

Raj Kumar Nair

d. Request for a Loan

Sample:

Sender's Address Line
Phone Number/Email Address
Account Number
Date

Roop Kumar Trivedi
Customer Service Manager

Western Bank Limited
1B, Greater Kailash Part II
New Delhi – 110 012

Dear Sir,

I would like to apply for a Home Loan of ₹ 5,00,000 only from your bank for extension and addition to my existing property.

I would like to pay back the loan in 60 equal monthly installments at your prescribed interest rate.

At present I am employed with City Transport Corporation Limited as a Manager and have been working with the company for last 15 years. I have not taken a loan earlier and my property is not mortgaged to any bank.

Copies of my bank statements, credit card bills and a salary certificate from my employer are enclosed herewith for your perusal.

I would be grateful for an appointment with you for further discussion in the matter.

Yours faithfully,

Signature

R.S. Unnikrishnan

2. DISCREPANCY LETTERS

These are letters pointing out discrepancy in accounting or billing and highlight errors in statements or bank balance. These are extremely important letters which must be preserved in case any dispute arises between the consumer and the bank in question. Customers usually scan through their billing statement carefully to ensure that there is no error in billing. At times billing errors take place due to wrong entry or a faulty computer system. As soon as the error is detected, banks should be notified so that they can make an immediate rectification. The letter should:

- Request for particular information regarding the error
- Request for immediate rectification of the error
- Ask for a new bank statement
- Give contact information
- Mention the account number

a. Discrepancy in Transaction

Sample:

Sender's Address Line
Phone Number/Email Address
Account Number
Date

Roop Kumar Trivedi
Customer Service Manager
Western Bank Limited
1B, Greater Kailash Part II
New Delhi – 110 012

Dear Sir,

The statement of account for the month of May 2013, indicates a balance of ₹ 2,00,000 in my savings bank account. This does not tally with my record, showing a discrepancy of ₹ 20,000. You have debited my account with ₹ 20,000/- against the payment of a credit card bill on 7 May 2013.

I would like to point out that I do not hold any credit card from your bank and did not issue any cheque towards any payment of the bill.

Please instruct your Accounts Department to cross-check the above information in their records and rectify the error urgently. Please send me a revised bank statement without any delay.

Prompt action in the matter would be highly appreciated.

Yours faithfully,

Signature

Joy Khurana

To: roop.trivedi@westernbankindia.com
Subject: Discrepancy in Transaction

Name:
Account No:

Dear Sir,

The statement of account for the month of May 2013, indicates a balance of ₹ 2,00,000 in my savings bank account. This does not tally with my record, showing a discrepancy of ₹ 20,000. You have debited my account with ₹ 20,000/- against the payment of a credit card bill on 7 May 2013.

I would like to point out that I do not hold any credit card from your bank and did not issue any cheque towards any payment of the bill.

Please instruct your Accounts Department to cross-check the above information in their records and rectify the error urgently. Please send me a revised bank statement without any delay.

Prompt action in the matter would be highly appreciated.

Yours faithfully,

Joy Khurana

Email Signature Line

b. Billing Error

Sample:

Sender's Address Line
Phone Number/Email Address
Account Number
Date

Mr Arun Singh
Manager
Customer Service Department
East West Bank
25, Barakhamba Road
New Delhi – 110 011

Dear Sir,

Your billing statement for the month of September has just been received by me. After going through it carefully, I find that I have been credited with ₹ 20,000/- paid for purchases in Shopper Square, Greater Noida on 22 September 2013. I would like to point out that I never made any purchases from that particular shop on the date mentioned. It seems that a billing error has taken place due to wrong entry into my account.

Please check it carefully and reconcile my account balance as soon as possible.

I am returning the statement and will make the payment as and when I get the corrected statement.

Your early action to rectify the error will be highly appreciated.

Thanking you,

Signature

Naina Malhotra

3. LETTER TO CLOSE AN ACCOUNT

This kind of letter should be short and precise and clearly mention details like name, address and account number. It should also mention the branch and stress on immediacy of the closure.

Sample:

Sender's Address Line
Phone Number/Email Address
Account Number
Date

Manager
Eastern Indian Bank
24, Sarat Bose Road Branch
Kolkata – 700 029

Dear Sir,

I would like to close my savings bank account with you with immediate effect as I have been transferred to Delhi and will be shifting out of Kolkata shortly. The details of my account are as follows:

Name: Randeep Sood
Savings Account No: 00025910

Please prepare a cheque for the amount lying in my account after adjusting any charges, if applicable. I will collect the cheque from your Gariahat branch after your confirmation. I shall also hand over the Debit ATM card and the unused cheque book to you at that time.

Please accept my thanks for the excellent services rendered.

Yours faithfully,

Signature

Randeep Sood

4. APPLICATION FOR A BANK LOCKER

Sample:

Sender's Address Line
Phone Number/Email Address
Account Number
Date

Senior Manager
Customer Services Department
Universal Bank Limited
Ballard Estate Branch
25, Ballard Estate
Mumbai – 400 036

Dear Sir,

I have been a customer of your bank for last 15 years. Last month I have opened a fixed deposit account with ₹ 20,00,000. As per your specification the facility of a bank locker is available to me. Kindly allot me a locker to be held jointly by my wife and myself.

Relevant details as required by you for allotting the locker are given below:

Name – Nirmal Sharma
Type of Account – Savings Account
Account No – SB 33095

Fixed Deposit No – FD S44999
Name of Holders – Nirmal Sharma and Pragati Sharma
Amount of FD – ₹ 20,00,000

Looking forward to your prompt action in this regard.

Thanking you,

Signature

Nirmal Sharma

5. NOTIFICATION OF CHANGE OF ADDRESS

This kind of letter should have the address marked out in bold as well as an attention line at the top of the letter. It should also have the account number and any other related information like credit card numbers should also be mentioned so that all the related correspondence from the bank is delivered to your new address.

Sample:

Sender's Address Line
Phone Number/Email Address
Account Number
Date

Senior Manager
Customer Services Department
Town Bank
22, August Kranti Marg
Mumbai – 400 036

Dear Sir,

Change of Address

Samrat Sen
Savings Bank Account No SB S77123
VISA Credit Card No 1123 4484 3352 9998

I have recently shifted from my residence 39, August Kranti Marg, Flat No 3, Mumbai – 400 036 to my present address – **Flat No. 4A, Deodar Apartment, 99, Antop Hill, Mumbai – 400 037.**

Two copies of my proof of residence are also attached herewith.

I would request to you to please amend my address in your books with immediate effect and send all future communication to my present address.

Please instruct your concerned department accordingly and a line in confirmation will be highly appreciated.

Thanking you,

Signature

Samrat Sen

6. REQUESTING A CHEQUEBOOK

Sample:

Sender's Address Line
Phone Number/Email Address
Account Number
Date

Senior Manager
Customer Services Department
Town Bank
22, August Kranti Marg
Mumbai – 400 036

Dear Sir,

Requisition for a New Chequebook

Please issue me a new cheque book containing 100 cheques to the bearer of this letter, Mr Arjun Singh, whose signature is attested below. The requisition slip, duly signed, is attached herewith.

Please debit my account with the charges for issuance of chequebook, as applicable.

Thanking you,

Signature

Abhinab Sahai

____

(Signature of Arjun Singh)

ATTESTED

____

(Signature of Abhinab Sahai)

7. UNAUTHORIZED CREDIT CARD CHARGE

This type of letter which informs the bank of an unauthorized charge that has been issued from their end, must be very clear mentioning all the dates, amounts and earlier correspondence to prove the consumer's point.

Sample:

Sender's Address Line
Phone Number/Email Address
Account Number
Date

Senior Manager
Customer Services Department
Town Bank
22, August Kranti Marg
Mumbai – 400 036

Dear Sir,

I am in receipt of my credit card bill for the month of September, 2013. I would like to point out some discrepancy regarding unauthorized charges made by you.

You offered me the optional insurance facility by your circular letter dated 23 August 2013. The monthly premium was ₹ 1000 for a total insured amount of ₹ 5,00,000. I categorically refused the offer through a letter dated 5 September 2013 to you.

I am surprised to find that in spite of my refusal, the first premium of ₹ 1000 has been added to my current bill which is unacceptable to me. I have not made the payment of this bill. Please issue the revised bill on an urgent basis so that it can be paid within the due date without attracting any penalty.

Your prompt action will be highly appreciated.

Thanking you,

Signature

Swarnanand Singh

8. REQUESTING AN ADD-ON CREDIT CARD

Sample:

Sender's Address Line
Phone Number/Email Address
Account/Credit Card Number
Date

Senior Manager
Credit Card Division
Town Bank
22, August Kranti Marg
Mumbai – 400 036

Dear Sir,

Please add my son's name Kushan Singh to my Visa Gold credit card account and issue him an add-on card at the earliest possible. He is going off to college in Delhi this summer and a credit card would be of great use during emergencies.

I have been a preferred customer of your bank for the last 10 years and I think my credit card account allows me to have up to three add-on cards in my name. The bills will obviously continue coming to me on a monthly basis for their due payment.

I look forward to hearing from you at the earliest possible.

Thanking you,

Signature

Swarnanand Singh

9. REQUEST FOR AN INCREASE IN CREDIT LIMIT

Sample:

Sender's Address Line
Phone Number/Email Address
Account/Credit Card Number
Date

Senior Manager
Credit Card Division
Town Bank
22, August Kranti Marg
Mumbai – 400 036

Dear Sir,

I would like to increase my current credit limit on my Visa Platinum Card no xxxx4567 from ₹ 2,00,000 to 3,00,000 with immediate effect. I am going to be travelling to Europe next month and would like a ready credit card with a substantial limit for any expenses incurred while travelling.

I have been a preferred customer of your bank for the last 10 years and I think my credit card history has been very good till date with timely payment of high value bills.

I hope you revert at the earliest.

Thanking you,

Signature

Swarnanand Singh

10. WRONG INVOICE CHARGED TO THE CREDIT CARD

Sample:

Sender's Address Line
Phone Number/Email Address
Account/Credit Card Number
Date

Senior Manager
Customer Services Department
Town Bank
22, August Kranti Marg
Mumbai – 400 036

Dear Sir,

This has reference to the credit card bill for the month of September 2013. After scanning through the bill I noticed that an amount of ₹ 15,000 spent on purchase of goods in East Side Dresses on 23 September 2013, has been included in my bill.

I would like to mention that the above purchase was not made by me. Please check your records and I am sure you would find this a wrong entry inadvertently added to my bill.

I am returning the aforesaid bill for your rectification. Please send the revised bill soon so I can pay within the due date.

Thanking you,

Signature

Swarnanand Singh

11. LETTERS TO INSURANCE COMPANIES:

Insurance letters should be courteous, formal and assertive. Here are the main features for an effective claim letter:

- Clearly specify the type of claim
- Mention the policy and other important reference numbers
- Clearly mention the amount of the claim
- All the relevant documents should be enclosed with the claim
- Claim should be sent within the particular time frame

a. Letter to Insurance Company Requesting a Policy

Sample:

Sender's Address Line
Phone Number/Email Address
Date

Kuntal Bose
Manager (New Policies)
ANC Insurance Company Limited
34, BBD Bag
Kolkata – 700 001

Dear Sir,

Car Insurance

I would like to insure my brand new Toyota Innova VX variant which will be delivered by the first week of May 2013, with your company.

Please provide me with the details of the terms and conditions for a comprehensive policy along with the necessary forms and information on the premiums payable from my side.

I will provide you with all the necessary documents after hearing from you.

An early response will be highly appreciated.

Thanking you,

Signature

Rishav Sen

To: kuntal.bose@ANCindia.com
Subject: Request for Car Insurance Policy

Dear Sir,

I would like to insure my brand new Toyota Innova VX variant which will be delivered by the first week of May 2013, with your company.

Please provide me with the details of the terms and conditions for a comprehensive policy along with the necessary forms and information on the premiums payable from my side.

I will provide you with all the necessary documents after hearing from you.

An early response will be highly appreciated.

Thanking you,

Rishav Sen

Email Signature Line

b. Insurance Claim against Hospitalization

Sample:

Sender's Address Line
Phone Number/Email Address
Date

Medical Claim Department
Horizon Insurance Company Limited
269, Theatre Road
Kolkata – 700 017

Dear Sirs,

Mayur Raina
Date of Birth – 22-01-1990
Policy No MR-90-205
Medical Claim

My son Mayur was suffering from jaundice since June 30 2013. He was advised hospitalization by our medical specialist and was accordingly admitted to the Springtime Nursing Home on 9 July 2013. He was released on 30 July 2013.

I am enclosing herewith nursing home bills, bills for the medicines and the doctors' consultation fees. A copy of the policy is also enclosed for your ready reference.

I would request you for an early reimbursement of my claim against the above policy.

Please let me know if any other documents are required by you in this respect.

Thanking you,

Signature

Manoj Raina

c. Insurance Claim against Death

Sample:

Sender's Address Line
Phone Number/Email Address
Date

Life Insurance Department
Horizon Insurance Company Limited
269, Theatre Road
Kolkata – 700 017

Dear Sirs,

Ankita Ramani
Date of Birth – 13-11-1957
Policy No AR-Life-19880
Life Insurance

I regret to inform you that my wife Mrs Ankita Ramani expired on 1 August 2013, after a prolonged illness. Her life was insured under the above policy for an amount of ₹ 20,00,000. A copy of her death certificate issued by a registered medical practitioner is attached herewith.

As the sole nominee of my late wife's policy, I am forwarding the claim for remittance of the insured amount of ₹ 20,00,000 though nothing can compensate for this irreparable loss. The life insurance policy in original is attached herewith.

An early settlement of the claim would be highly appreciated.

Yours faithfully,

Signature

Sitaram Ramani

d. Insurance Claim for Fire Insurance

Sample:

Sender's Address Line
Phone Number/Email Address
Date

Horizon Insurance Company Limited
Fire Insurance Claim Department
269, Theatre Road
Kolkata – 700 017

Dear Sirs,

Fire Insurance Policy No AF-79211

I regret to inform you on the 29 July 2013 a devastating fire broke out in my premises No 224, Kyd Street, Kolkata – 700 013. The building was seriously damaged by the intensive blaze. The interior of the building was totally gutted. We have lost all our household items in the fire. The fire brigade came within 10 minutes and brought the fire in control after two hours. Their quick action saved the structure from collapsing.

My house was insured against fire accidents for a sum of ₹ 80 lakh (Policy No. AF-79211 dated 2 January 2005). All the premiums have been paid up to to date.

We estimate the loss around ₹ 40 lakh and would request you to please depute your surveyor to assess the damage caused by the fire. Please also let us know about the formalities to be complied with regard to the claim.

Looking forward to your prompt action in the matter.

Thanking you,

Signature

Virat Taneja

Complaint Letters

Written complaints are a much better way to communicate your grievances and more effective in the long run. Complaint letters are a powerful way to express a customer's/consumer's dissatisfaction with a particular product or service. Written complaints carry far more weight than a verbal complaint since records are essential for further action, if necessary.

A complaint letter should be short and specific and should end with a positive note. If remedial action is required then a time frame should be mentioned in a polite yet firm manner.

Complaint letters should be:

- Addressed to the appropriate person or department
- Brief and to the point
- Factual
- Polite
- Mention a time limit
- In extreme cases they should also mention some kind of punitive measures

1. LETTERS TO CUSTOMER SERVICE FOR RUDE BEHAVIOUR

a. Letters to Airlines Customer Service for Rude Behaviour of Staff

Sample:

Sender's Address Line
Phone Number/Email Address
Date

Customer Service Manager
Green Airways Limited
23, Barakhamba Road
New Delhi – 110 011

Dear Sir,

Rude Behaviour of your Staff

I would like to draw your kind attention to the unexpected rude behaviour of your ground staff.

I have been flying with your Silk Wings Airlines for the last 10 years regularly and this is the first time I have had such an unpleasant experience. I was booked on Business Class for the Delhi-Bangalore Flight No SWA 423 scheduled to depart at 2.30 p.m. I was supposed to report by 1 p.m. to your counter for checking in. Due to sudden rain and the resultant traffic jam, I got delayed and reached the airport at 1.15 p.m. As soon as I reached the counter, I apologized to your staff for the delay and explained the situation. But the lady at the counter whose name was Priya Virmani, summarily dismissed me by giving her verdict that I was too late for my flight and the counter was closed. She had a very rude and unprofessional attitude. Now I know that the counter shuts 45 minutes before departure and I had already completed a web check-in. The process should have been smooth as there more than enough time at hand. Yet, your staff member refused to listen to me and as a result wasted more time. As there was no other option, I ran around looking for a more senior member of the airlines to help me out. After much trouble, I was able to locate a supervisor who sorted out the matter and allowed me to take the flight. However, the whole incident was very unpleasant and stressful and caused me to nearly miss my flight even though I was at the airport 1 hour and 15 minutes prior to the departure time.

This kind of behaviour is unacceptable from a reputed airline service like yours. Your staff is there to help the passengers not to create problems for them. I would request you to please ensure that your staff is instructed to deal with the passengers in a courteous manner in the near future.

I would appreciate an acknowledgement of my letter.

Thanking you,

Signature

Raghavendra Raghavan

b. Letters to Railways Customer Service for Rude Behaviour of Staff

Sample:

Sender's Address Line
Phone Number/Email Address
Date

Manager
Customer Service
Eastern Railways
Howrah

Dear Sir,

<u>Rude Behaviour of Railway Staff</u>

Indian Railways are well known for their hospitality and excellent service provided to all passengers. The warm and helpful approach of the staff makes the journey a pleasant experience. I travel between Delhi and Kolkata by Rajdhani Express very often and enjoy the superb service and good food. However, my recent experience was quite unpleasant and has compelled me to bring it to your attention.

I was travelling from Delhi to Kolkata by Rajdhani Express on 21 September 2013 and everything was fine till we reached Gaya. Soon after the train left Gaya, the AC started malfunctioning and as a result the compartment became very uncomfortable and claustrophobic. I complained to one of the attendants on duty called Manish Yadav but there was no effect. Unable to bear the heat, I asked him about it again after one hour. Instead of placating me and other uncomfortable passengers, he just flared up and spoke to me in a very rude manner. It was unexpected and without any provocation. I kept quiet as I did not want to get into an argument with him. When the Ticket Examiner came to check our tickets, I complained to him and he informed the higher authorities about the AC. Soon after that it was rectified.

I feel all passengers should be treated with respect. Your staff should be instructed to be civil and well mannered towards the passengers so that incidents like these do not mar the travel experience on the very good Rajdhani trains.

I would appreciate an acknowledgement of my letter.

Thanking you,

Signature

Raman Khera

2. LETTERS TO CUSTOMER SERVICE FOR BAD FOOD AND POOR HYGIENE

a. Letter to Restaurant Customer service for Bad Food

Sample:

Sender's Address Line
Phone Number/Email Address
Date

Manager
Customer Help Desk
Mughal Garden Restaurant
Chirag International Hotel
25, Connaught Place
New Delhi – 110 001

Dear Sir,

I visited the Mughal Garden Restaurant at the Chirag International Hotel, Gurgaon branch, with my wife on 24 October 2013 to celebrate our marriage anniversary. I have been a regular patron of your CP branch for many years now and was expecting the same high standards from your newly-opened branch in Gurgaon. Unfortunately your food was not up to the mark and some of your signature dishes were stale and unpalatable.

We ordered the Chicken Reshmi Kabab and Tandoori Prawns as starters, which are usually very tasty and melt in your mouth. However, this time they turned out to be tasteless and very hard, especially the prawns which were stale and had an unpleasant smell. We could not eat them and practically left it untouched. When we asked the waiter to replace our dish, he refused to believe that it was stale and as a result it was wasted.

The main course did not fare any better. We asked for an array of non-vegetarian and vegetarian dishes. Surprisingly, all the dishes tasted more or less the same and were bland, insipid and lukewarm. It seemed as if the same gravy had been used for all the dishes. We hardly enjoyed our dinner and wasted most of it.

We were so disappointed with your food that we did not dare to order dessert and went to another restaurant instead.

Your restaurant has always been famous for its quality of food and good service. Though we have no complaints about the service, the same cannot be said about the food. The same brand name cannot be so inconsistent across the city and that too in a new location. This is the first time that the food in Mughal Garden Restaurant was so disappointing. Please ensure that your chefs in all your branches are equally trained and that the quality of food matches up to your reputation.

Best regards,

Signature

Nimesh Talwar

b. Letter to International Fast Food Chain Customer Service for Poor Hygiene

Sample:

Sender's Address Line
Phone Number/Email Address
Date

Manager
Customer Service
Super Sandwiches
29, Airport Road
Bangalore – 560 059

Dear Sir,

My family and I went to the Super Sandwiches Jayanagar outlet for dinner on 23 September 2013 around 8 p.m. We ordered American Hot Dogs and Chicken Mayo Sandwiches. The food was served promptly. After a few bites of the hot dog, I felt some foreign object in my mouth which tasted strange. I investigated further to see that there was a whole soiled band-aid in my hot dog. It was absolutely disgusting and both me and my family immediately lost our appetites and no one touched any of the food we had ordered.

We immediately complained to your manager who was most unapologetic and instead, tried to accuse us of putting the band-aid in the sandwich! We were so appalled by his behavior that we immediately left the restaurant after paying for our uneaten meal. Not only was it a matter of poor hygiene, it is also the shocking behavior of your manager that has led me to file this complaint. We could have fallen sick from the contaminated band-aid and it is hardly something one would expect of an international chain like yours. Furthermore, there wasn't a single apology that came our way after this disastrous meal.

I hope you will take immediate steps to improve the hygiene of your restaurant as well as correct the behaviour of your staff.

Looking forward to your prompt action.

Regards

Signature

Raghav Singh

To: customercare@supersandwichindia.com
Subject: Complaint for Poor Hygiene and Rude Staff

Dear Sir,

My family and I went to the Super Sandwiches Jayanagar outlet for dinner on 23 September 2013 around 8 p.m. We ordered American Hot Dogs and Chicken Mayo Sandwiches. The food was served promptly. After a few bites of the hot dog, I felt some foreign object in my mouth which tasted strange. I investigated further to see that there was a whole soiled band-aid in my hot dog. It was absolutely disgusting and both me and my family immediately lost our appetites and no one touched any of the food we had ordered.

We immediately complained to your manager who was most unapologetic and instead, tried to accuse us of putting the band-aid in the sandwich! We were so appalled by his behavior that we immediately left the restaurant after paying for our uneaten meal. Not only was it a matter of poor hygiene, it is also the shocking behavior of your manager that has led me to file this complaint. We could have fallen sick from the contaminated band-aid and it is hardly something one would expect of an international chain like yours. Furthermore, there wasn't a single apology that came our way after this disastrous meal.

I hope you will take immediate steps to improve the hygiene of your restaurant as well as correct the behaviour of your staff.

Looking forward to your prompt action.

Regards

Raghav Singh
Email Signature Line

3. LETTERS TO CUSTOMER SERVICE FOR BAD SERVICE

a. Letter to ABCL Cable Customer Service regarding a Problem with the Cable Connection

Sender's Address Line
Phone Number/Email Address
Date

Customer Service Dept
ACPL Cable Service
23, Lake Road
Kolkata – 700 029

Dear Sirs,

I have been an ACPL customer for the last five years. I would like to draw your attention to the problems I have been having in the recent past. My cable connection gets disconnected at least thrice a week around the same time every evening between 8 p.m. and 10 p.m. This is really annoying as this is prime-time television when all the important news-related programmes and television serials are on. It is very difficult to get in touch with your customer service number which is supposed to be a 24-hour service and even if someone does take the call and register the complaint – nothing is done in a hurry. It takes at least two hours before the cable connection comes back and we end up missing most of the good programmes aired during this time.

You promised uninterrupted transmission during the installation. For the first few years your service was really good. We had good quality HD transmission and there was no disturbance in service. However, in the last couple of months your service is going from bad to worse. Your server seems to be malfunctioning very often and even the slightest hint of rain causes the connection to go off. In spite of all these problems, your subscription fee has been increasing every year by a substantial amount.

I would request you to improve your service as soon as possible, otherwise I will have no other option but to discontinue with your cable network.

Looking forward to a positive response.

Thanking you,

Signature

Manajit Bera

b. Letter to Data A1 Internet Customer Service regarding Problems with the Internet Connection

Sample:

Sender's Address Line
Phone Number/Email Address
Date

Manager
Customer Care
Quick Tel Limited
35, Senapati Bapat Marg
Lower Parel
Mumbai – 400 013

Dear Sir,

I had subscribed to your Unlimited Download Programme for ₹ 1099 per month in April 2013. I am not at all happy with your service and would like to point out the problems I am facing.

Your server is very slow and it takes 10–15 minutes for any website to open. Very often while I am downloading some important information it gets disconnected and I have to start from the scratch again – this is a very time-consuming process and it hampers my work.

At times the Internet does not connect at all and it keeps displaying the message 'Server is Down. Please contact your Service Provider,' on the screen. After a series of complaints, your representative visited my house and changed the modem, but even after that there seems to have been no marked improvement.

I am writing to you as a last resort since the verbal complaints over the phone do not produce any fruitful results. I would request you to look into the problem and provide me with an uninterrupted and speedy internet connection without any further delay. If this is not possible then I would like to withdraw my subscription and look for another service provider.

A line in confirmation would be highly appreciated.

Best regards

Signature

Rajiv Deshmukh

4. COMPLAINT LETTERS ABOUT PRODUCTS

a. Complaint Letter about Incomplete Delivery of Products

Sample:

Sender's Address Line
Phone Number/Email Address
Date

Mr Nilkant Mohta
Senior Sales Executive
Electronics Industries Limited
202, Park Street
Kolkata – 700 017

Dear Sir,

This has reference to our order letter dated 10 May 2013, placing an order for 20 close circuit monitors with cables for the purpose of internal security of our organization. The monitors have been delivered without the cables on 17 May 2013. We pointed out the mistake immediately and even after numerous verbal and written complaints, we still have not received the full consignments although your bills have arrived. Due to non-availability of the cables we cannot introduce our new security operations.

We request you to please deliver the cables without further delay as it is hampering our security network.

We are withholding payment of your bill until the cables are supplied and our system becomes operative.

An early response to resolve the matter will be appreciated.

Yours faithfully,

Suraj Rathi
Manager (Purchase)

b. Complaint Letter about Faulty Product

Sender's Address Line
Phone Number/Email Address
Date

Mr Raghav Bhandari
Senior Customer Services Manager
Brilliant Gadgets Limited
23, Budge Budge Road
Kolkata – 700 027

Dear Sir,

I had purchased the Automatic Washing Machine EX-134 from your company – receipt no 24533 dated 2 May 2013. Your engineer came and gave me a demonstration of the machine and installed it the next day itself. Within a week, the washing machine started malfunctioning. I informed your service department and your service engineer came and inspected the machine and failed to rectify the defect. He certified that the machine was a defective piece and since it was obviously within the warranty period he would inform the company and make sure that it was replaced free of cost.

After six weeks and twice as many telephone calls, a replacement washing machine has not been delivered and my current machine has stopped working altogether. I am tired of waiting and following up with your company. I am really disappointed with your products and after-sales service and I am writing this letter hoping for some redressal.

I would request you to take prompt action otherwise I would have no other option but to ask for a refund.

I trust the matter will be solved amicably.

Yours faithfully,

Signature

Neeraj Singh

To: customercare@brilliantgadgetsindia.com
Subject: Complaint about Newly Purchased Faulty Washing Machine

Dear Sir,

I had purchased the Automatic Washing Machine EX-134 from your company – receipt no 24533 dated 2 May 2013. Your engineer came and gave me a demonstration of the machine and installed it the next day itself. Within a week, the washing machine started malfunctioning. I informed your service department and your service engineer came and inspected the machine and failed to rectify the defect. He certified that the machine was a defective piece and since it was obviously within the warranty period he would inform the company and make sure that it was replaced free of cost.

After six weeks and twice as many telephone calls, a replacement washing machine has not been delivered and my current machine has stopped working altogether. I am tired of waiting and following up with your company. I am really disappointed with your products and after-sales service and I am writing this letter hoping for some redressal.

I would request you to take prompt action otherwise I would have no other option but to ask for a refund.

I trust the matter will be solved amicably.

Yours faithfully,

Neeraj Singh

Email Signature Line

c. Complaint Letter about Defective Workmanship

Sender's Address Line
Phone Number/Email Address
Date

Mr Samar Mitra
Customer Service Executive
Comforts Shoe Limited
22, Brabourne Road
Kolkata – 700 001

Dear Sir,

I purchased a pair of Comfort Power Shoes on 2 June 2013, from your Park Street outlet. The product code was CP-22. After using the shoes for barely one week, the soles have come apart and cracks have started appearing on top of the shoes.

I went back to your outlet with the bill and the shoes and lodged a complaint. The salespeople expressed their apologies but also said that there were unable to replace the shoes as they had been used. I was advised to send a written complaint along with the bills to your head office on Brabourne Road. The manager of the Park Street store also said that further action would be taken as per the head office's instructions.

Subsequently I wrote to your head office on 16 June 2013, enclosing the original bill and I am yet to receive a reply. I would like to know the following things:

a. Why are such substandard products sold by a reputed brand such as yours?
b. Why they are not replaced immediately? Why does it take more than a month to sort out something that is obviously a genuine manufacturing defect?
c. How are such products approved by your quality-control department?

Under the circumstances I would request you to either replace the shoes immediately or give me a full refund.

A copy of my letter dated 16 June, written to your head office along with a copy of the purchase invoice is enclosed.

Your quick action will be highly appreciated

Warm regards

Signature

Anupam Auddy

5. COMPLAINT LETTERS ABOUT LATE DELIVERY

Sample:

Company Letterhead

Date

Mr Mudit Bahadur
General Manager (Supplies)
Insulated Cable Company Limited
35, Taratalla Road
Kolkata – 700 027

Dear Sir,

We would like to draw your attention to our Purchase Order dated 26 May 2013, for supply of 9000 metres of insulated cables. You mentioned in your initial quotation to us that the goods would be supplied within two weeks. However, nearly two months have passed and we have received nothing from your end, and neither have we been given any intimation about the delivery date. Due to this delay our production schedule is being hampered and this is causing lot of inconvenience to our customers.

Under the circumstances, we have no other option but to ask you to deliver the goods positively within a week, or the order will stand cancelled from our end without any further intimation.

Your immediate action would be appreciated.

Yours faithfully,

Signature

Umed Desai

6. EMPLOYEE COMPLAINT LETTERS ABOUT COMPANY ADMINISTRATION

Company Letterhead

Date

Mr Rohit Puri
General Manager (HRD)
Time Machines Limited
Electronic City, Salt Lake
Kolkata – 700 091

Dear Sir,

We would like to inform you that the cooling plant in the System Management Department is not functioning properly for last two weeks. The employees of this department are facing a lot of inconvenience due to the heat and high levels of humidity. This is affecting people's health and temperament and the overall performance levels are going down.

The malfunctioning cooling system is also affecting our computer systems. As you know, the server is located on our floor and requires a certain temperature to function properly. Although the server room is cooler than our space, it is still warmer than the ideal recommended temperature for these sensitive machines.

The generator has also been acting up and there have been frequent breakdowns which have caused loss of data. This in turn has increased the work load of the employees.

Adverse working conditions teamed with the system failure are creating discontent among the employees and also affecting the company's productivity.

We have spoken to the concerned department a number of times, but so far no action has been taken. We feel that the convenience of the workers should be given priority.

We would request you to look into the problem and solve the matter soon.

Thanking you,

Signature

Amber Raj
Systems Manager

7. EMPLOYEE COMPLAINT (SEXUAL HARASSMENT)

This kind of letter broaches a very sensitive and controversial matter in the workplace and must be framed very carefully as all the parties implicated could be liable to face legal proceedings. Letters of this kind should be:

- Detailed and clear mentioning all instances of harassment
- The language must be strict but not threatening

Sample:

Company Letterhead

Date

Mr Rohit Puri
General Manager (HRD)
Time Machines Limited
Electronic City, Salt Lake
Kolkata – 700 091

Dear Sir,

I am writing this letter as there is no other option but to apprise you of the situation where I have been a victim of sexual harassment by the departmental head.

He does not follow the office decorum. He wants to exploit his position. On several occasions, he has made indecent comments tinged with sexual overtones. Last evening at the departmental get-together, he crossed all limits and asked me to go home with him at night. This is beyond my tolerance level.

I have been working in this company for the last five years and I have never experienced this kind of problem before. I have been treated with dignity and respect by all my colleagues till now. The company's policy is to create an atmosphere that is conducive to professional growth, equality and mutual respect for each other. His behaviour is a contradiction to all that the company believes in.

Please keep my complaint in strict confidence and take necessary action in the matter.

Regards,

Signature

Sumitra Khera
Public Relations Officer

8. CANCELLATION LETTER FOR A PRODUCT OR SERVICE

Cancellation letters are brief and clear-cut. The cause of cancellation should be mentioned clearly and the letter should end in a gracious manner. This is also a complaint letter as the cancellation is obviously in response to miscommunication and an oversight on the service provider's part. These letters should mention:

- Order number
- Date
- All instances of prior communication

Sample:

Sender's Address Line
Phone Number/Email Address
Date

Manager (Consumer Products)
Sweet Home Appliances Limited
309, Electronics City
Pardesipura
Indore – 542 010

Dear Sir,

Order for –
1) Mixer-Grinder-Juicer
2) Electric Kettle
3) Electric Sandwich Toaster

This has reference to my letter dated 16 June 2013, placing an order for the above-mentioned items under your Puja Special Discount Scheme valid till 30 June. Under the above scheme I was entitled to 20% discount on the products. I received your confirmation of my order in writing on 25 June 2013.

I have been dealing with your company for the last 10 years and your products were always of the best quality and the service was prompt and courteous, until now.

The items were delivered on 16 July and I was charged full price without the promised discount. I refused to take delivery and sent them back as I was buying the items under a special deal. I called your customer service helpline and pointed out the discrepancy in the price. However, your excutive refused to listen to me and stated that the discount period was over and that I was not entitled to any price reduction.

I cannot accept the goods at the revised price and I would request you to please resolve the matter quickly, or cancel my order.

Thanking you,

Signature

Manohar Mukherjee

9. RESPONSES TO COMPLAINT LETTERS

These letters should be extremely polite and should address the customer's issues and try to resolve the matter as amicably as possible as the company or individual service provider's reputation is at stake.

a. Response to Complaint about Faulty Product

Sample:

Company Letterhead

Date

Mr Neeraj Singh
22A, New Alipore
Kolkata – 700 027

Dear Sir,

With reference to your letter dated 15 July 2013, we note that you are not satisfied with our after-sales service. Our company usually prides itself for its excellent after-sales services. This is not part of our work culture and we are very sorry for the inconvenience caused to you.

In the meantime, we are sending our senior engineer for an inspection immediately and if the fault is not rectified to your satisfaction, we will replace the washing machine without any further delay.

Once again, please accept our sincere apology. If in future you ever experience any inconvenience relating to the service provided by our company, please contact the undersigned without any hesitation and we will take care of it on a priority basis.

Hope this meets with your approval.

Yours faithfully,

Signature

Raghav Bhandari
Senior Customer Services Manager

b. Response to Complaint about Late Delivery

Sample:

Company Letterhead

Date

Mr Umed Desai
General Manager (Purchase)
Eastern Telecom Limited
Garden Reach
Kolkata – 700 024

Dear Sir,

We are in receipt of your letter dated 22 July 2011, and we sincerely apologize for the inconvenience caused to you and the problems you faced with your customers due to our delayed delivery of goods.

Your goods have already been dispatched and it will be delivered to your factory by tomorrow. We will take great care that in future all your orders are dispatched as per the time schedule committed by us. This is the first time we gave you a reason for complaint and this was because we had a serious labour problem in our factory over the last month which had hampered our production. However, the matter has been resolved and normalcy is restored in our factory. This has created a backlog and due to this we have not been able to meet your requirements on time.

We are offering you an extra 5% discount for the inconvenience. Considering our long-standing business association, we hope this will be acceptable to you and our business relations will continue as earlier.

Yours faithfully,

Mudit Bahadur
General Manager (Purchase)

To: umed.desai@easterntelecomindia.com
Subject: Regarding Late Delivery of Goods

We are in receipt of your letter dated 22 July 2011, and we sincerely apologize for the inconvenience caused to you and the problems you faced with your customers due to our delayed delivery of goods.

Your goods have already been dispatched and it will be delivered to your factory by tomorrow. We will take great care that in future all your orders are dispatched as per the time schedule committed by us. This is the first time we gave you a reason for complaint and this was because we had a serious labour problem in our factory over the last month which had hampered our production. However, the matter has been resolved and normalcy is restored in our factory. This has created a backlog and due to this we have not been able to meet your requirements on time.

We are offering you an extra 5% discount for the inconvenience. Considering our long-standing business association, we hope this will be acceptable to you and our business relations will continue as earlier.

Yours faithfully,

Mudit Bahadur

Email Signature Line

Letters to Customers

In any consumer or customer-related business, communication with the customer is all-important and letters are the best way to inform and educate them about your brands and products as well as news, special offers, or seasonal sales and discounts. Apart from promotion and marketing, these letters are also extremely important to appease disgruntled customers and convince them of your intent to please.

Regardless of the complaints that might have been forwarded and the varying degrees of dissatisfaction, customer care officials must take great pains to draft the right kind of letter that will satisfy unhappy consumers and also offer them incentives to continue patronizing your products or services.

These letters should be written in such a way that it generates interests among the readers and motivates them to act on it. The tone should be extremely polite and eager to please, thereby convincing the customer of your good intent.

1. ANNOUNCEMENT OF BUSINESS NAME CHANGE

Sample:

Company Letterhead

Date

Sunshine Industries Limited
747/1, Anna Salai
Chennai – 600 002

Dear Sirs,

We are happy to announce that our company has acquired the Blue Bell Company with effect from 1 September 2013. The merger has boosted our company's financial standing and will help us to start new ventures. Keeping in mind our future growth, we have decided to rename this new entity, **United Blacktop and Bell Company.** Our address remains unchanged.

In future, please address all your communication to the new name. We appreciate dealing with you as you are one of our valued customers and hope this change will only enhance the scope of our business in the future.

In case you need any clarification, please contact the undersigned.

Yours faithfully,

Signature

Raghav Keshavan
Company Secretary

2. APOLOGY TO A CUSTOMER FOR AN ACCOUNTING ERROR

Apology letters are basically damage-control letters and written to rectify an error. An apology letter to a customer should be:

- Issued in a timely manner
- Well-crafted
- Polite and sincere
- Language should be to the point and simple

Sample:

Sender's Address Line
Phone Number/Email Address
Date

Mr Hemant Saxena
Flat No 4

330, Green Park
New Delhi – 110 023

Dear Sir,

Thank you for bringing to our attention the accounting error in your bank statement for the month of August 2013. Your salary was erroneously credited to another account.

We have since rectified the error and credited your account with ₹ 50,000 and have also added a percentage of interest for the delay in depositing the amount into your account. The error was due to a breakdown in our computer system.

We sincerely apologize for the inconvenience caused to you for the accounting error and assure you of our continued good service in the future.

Yours faithfully,

Signature

Rajaram Modi
Accounts Manager

3. NOTICE TO A CUSTOMER FOR A CHEQUE RETURNED DUE TO NON-SUFFICIENT FUNDS

Non-sufficient funds means there is not enough money in the account to honour the cheque. Banks usually write to the customer explaining the reason for returning the cheque. Such letters should mention the following points:

- Cause for returning the cheque
- Amount of service charge payable by the customer
- Mode of payment

Sample:

Company Letterhead

Date

General Manager (Finance)
Prithvi Cables Company Limited

255/1, CMG Road
Bangalore – 560 024

Dear Sir,

We would like to inform you that your cheque no 335674 dated 23 September 2013 from Universal Bank for ₹ 20,00,000 submitted to us in payment for the goods supplied to you against your purchase order no 331 dated 10 September 2013, has been returned by the bank for non-sufficient funds. This cheque cannot be presented to the bank again as it has already been dishonoured once.

We would ask you now to make the full payment of ₹ 20,00,000 in cash along with a service charge of 5% on the above amount for the returned cheque within 3 days of the receipt of this letter. Please send the same to our Senior Manager (Finance) at our head office at 1020, Commercial Street, Bangalore – 560 221.

Your cheque along with the note from bank is returned herewith.

In case you fail to settle this matter within one week from the receipt of this letter, we will have no other option but to initiate legal action against you for financial irregularities.

If you need any further clarification, please contact the undersigned immediately over telephone or by email.

We would appreciate your prompt action in the matter

Yours faithfully,

Signature

V.R.S. Lakhsman
General Manager (Finance)

4. LETTER OFFERING DISCOUNT FOR SPEEDY PAYMENTS

Sample:

Company Letterhead

Date

Essential Electrical Goods Limited

1020, Commercial Street
Bangalore – 560 221

Dear Sirs,

We are delighted to announce our new scheme 'Pay Fast and Save Money' for our valued customers. We have a long business association with you and thus you have been selected as one of our privileged customers to avail of the scheme.

We are offering a discount of 5% against goods purchased worth ₹ 50,00,000 and more and the payments should be made within a week of receiving the goods. Apart from the aforementioned discount, you will collect reward points which can be redeemed against foreign holidays and monthly offers from various lifestyle brands.

We hope you will avail of this attractive scheme. We are looking forward to your orders.

Yours faithfully,

Signature

General Manager (Sales)

To: orders@essentialelectricsindia.com
Subject: Discount Offer for Speedy Payments

Dear Sirs,

We are delighted to announce our new scheme 'Pay Fast and Save Money' for our valued customers. We have a long business association with you and thus you have been selected as one of our privileged customers to avail of the scheme.

We are offering a discount of 5% against goods purchased worth ₹ 50,00,000 and be made within a week of receiving the goods. Apart from the aforementioned discount, you will collect reward points which can be redeemed against foreign holidays and monthly offers from various lifestyle brands.

We hope you will avail of this attractive scheme. We are looking forward to your orders.

Yours faithfully,

General Manager (Sales)

Email Signature Line

5. LETTER THANKING A CUSTOMER FOR TIMELY PAYMENT

The aim of this type of letter is basically to thank the customers for honouring their commitment. The letter should end wishing a continued cordial business association with the customer.

Company Letterhead

Date

Senior Manager (Finance)
Green Star Apparels Limited
35, Andheri West
Mumbai – 400 069

Dear Sirs,

We have received your cheque for ₹ 35 lakh on 13 October 2013, against the goods supplied to you last week. We thank you for the prompt payment and also appreciate your commitment to our business needs.

We look forward to working with you in the future. We greatly value your patronage and wish for a long business association.

Thanking you,

Signature

Deputy General Manager (Finance)

6. LETTER ANNOUNCING LAUNCH OF NEW PRODUCTS

Sample:

Company Letterhead

Date

To All Customers,

We have great pleasure in informing you that we have procured the dealership of Eastend Electronics and will be the sole distributors of their Home Appliances Range, including television sets, washing machines, microwave ovens and mixer grinders, among others.

We are attaching a catalogue of these new products along with the price list for your perusal. We assure you of a prompt delivery within 3 days from the day of purchase with free installation and demonstration.

All orders placed within 15 July 2013, will get a 10% discount.

We look forward to your continued patronage.

Thanking you,

Signature

Rajat Singh
Manager

Legal Letters

This kind of letter should be well worded as it is a precursor to legal action and can be produced for evidence, or a settlement. The language should be formal and the letters should clearly mention all kinds of facts and figures relevant to the case. It is better to send these letters as hard copies with signatures as they carry more authority and can be produced in a court of law if needed.

1. CEASE AND DESIST LETTER TO COLLECTOR

These are legal letters and preferably should be written under the guidance of legal authority. If this letter is ignored, it might lead to legal proceedings.

Sample:

Sender's Address Line
Phone Number/Email Address
Date

Mr M. K. Singh
Industrial Security Company
299, M.G. Road
Kolkata – 700 006

Dear Sir,

On 29 July 2013, a representative from your organization contacted me over the telephone regarding non-payment of a credit card loan and demanded immediate payment. I was surprised to receive his call as my loan against my Visa Card No xxx554 had been paid in full six months ago. I have got the bank's acknowledgement receipt in connection with the final settlement of the loan and subsequently, I have closed all transactions on the card.

As per legal procedure, I would request you to provide me in writing the following information:

- Amount of unpaid loan and the interest details
- Proof of your demand in respect to non-payment
- Copy of loan document and payment details
- Details of your company to prove the authenticity to operate as a collector on behalf of the bank

In the meantime, I am writing to my credit card company to point out the discrepancy and get the records corrected.

Please cease and desist from contacting me before you produce the above-mentioned information and confirm that you are stopping all your efforts to collect money which I do not owe the bank. If you fail to do so, I will have no other option but to start legal proceedings against you.

Yours faithfully,

Signature

Raghav Singhi

2. LETTERS INFORMING COMPANY ABOUT COPYRIGHT INFRINGEMENT

Copyright is a law which protects the rights of authors, artists, sculptors, architects and anyone else who creates something original regarding the right of reproduction, adaptation or translation. This law ensures that the creators should have exclusive rights over their creation and it cannot be reproduced without the owners' permission. In the event of infringement, the copyright owners can resort to legal action by way of injunction and sue for damages. It is a criminal offence and letters issued against copyright infringement should be carefully drafted as they can be followed up with legal action. Tips for writing a copyright infringement letter:

- Identification of the infringement
- Mention remedy of the situation

- Keep the tone very strict
- Specify a time limit for response, failing which legal action will be taken

a. Copyright Infringement Complaint by a Publishing Company

Company Letterhead

Date

Mr Akshay Yadav
22, Budge Budge Trunk Road
Kolkata – 700 027

Dear Sir,

We hold the copyright to all the information and illustrations printed in the book *A New Approach to General Science* published in May 2009. The book is a result of extensive research by our team and has been a bestselling text book since its release.

We have recently observed that your book *General Scientific Data* published in 2013, is very similar to the above-mentioned book. The chapters on, Mechanics, and, Electrical Energy, along with illustrations on pages 25, 38, 54, 116, 145, 165, 212 have been directly copied from our published text.

Since we have not granted any permission or licenses to anyone to reproduce our book and your company has published the same without any consultation with us, we hold you liable for infringement of our copyright. As per the Indian Copyright Law, we are entitled to an injunction against your act of infringement. We will also file a case for recovery of damages for the losses we have suffered due to your violation of the copyright law.

We demand that you do the following at the earliest possible:

- Remove all infringing materials from your book and notify us in writing of the same along with a copy of the book for approval before printing.
- Withdraw all your existing books from the market.
- Destroy all unsold copies of the book.

We would appreciate your immediate response to our letter otherwise we will have to resort to legal action without further intimation to you.

Yours faithfully,

Mangal Singh
Publishing Director

b. Copyright Infringement Complaint by an Individual

Sample:

Sender's Address Line
Phone Number/Email Address
Date

Mr Akshay Yadav
22, Budge Budge Trunk Road
Kolkata – 700 027

Dear Sir,

I hold the copyright to all the information and illustrations printed in the book *The Birdwatcher's Guide to the Himalayas* published in May 1998, by Anvil Books. The book is a result of my extensive research over a span of 10 years and has been consistently selling among enthusiasts since its release.

I recently discovered that your book called *Birds of India* published in May 2013, has chapters which have been directly lifted from my book. The chapters on 'Migration Patterns' and 'Colouration of Birds' along with illustrations on pages 25, 38, 54, 116, 145, 165, 212 have been directly copied from my book.

Since, neither I nor my publishers have granted any permission or licenses to anyone to reproduce content from my book, and your company has gone ahead published the same without any consultation with us, I hold you liable for infringement of my copyright. As per the Indian Copyright Law, I am entitled to an injunction against your act of infringement. I will also file a case for recovery of damages for the losses I have suffered due to your violation of the copyright law.

I demand that you do the following at the earliest possible:

- Remove all infringing materials from your book and notify me in writing of the same along with a copy of the book for approval before printing.

- Withdraw all your existing books from the market
- Destroy all unsold copies of the book

I would appreciate your immediate response to my letter otherwise I will have to resort to legal action without further intimation to you.

Yours faithfully,

Signature

Karun Acharya

Formal Letters

Formal letters are those business letters that are slightly less constrained by language and style than the letters we have seen so far in this book and are usually written by individuals to institutions, organizations, or the government. These letters are equally important in terms of conveying important information, querying matters, as well as making complaints or applications. They can be a little more creative than standard business letters and can take on a more personal tone in order to make the point. However, the structure and format as well as closings are like those in a typical business letter.

These type of letters typically include letters to editors of newspapers, application letters to colleges, letters to schools, letters to the government and enquiry letters, among others.

1. LETTERS TO THE EDITOR

The most significant way to air personal views as well as criticize or applaud civic, governmental, legal and any other issues or agendas, as well as comment on published news articles, is through letters to the editors ofleading newspapers and magazines in the country. These letters should be issue-based, factually correct and to the point. They can relate to any contemporary topic and should not be biased against any religion or communities. The tone should be positive and not accusatory as that will reduce its chances of getting published.

Well-written letters, especially on online forums, can mobilize public opinion and even yield a response from the authorities in question.

The following points must be kept in mind while writing a letter to the editor:

- The letter should be short and tight. Try and keep the 400-word limit in mind.
- Get the reader's attention by immediately addressing the issue in the opening line itself.
- The letter must always mention the sender's name and full address.
- Address an issue by way of solutions and not criticism alone as this will make it an interesting letter to print.
- There is no need for a signature in a letter to an editor as only the sender's name is printed.

a. Letter Criticizing Strikes in the State

Sample 1:

Sender's Address Line
Date

Editor
The Daily Sun
22, Chandni Chowk
Kolkata – 700001

Dear Editor,

There has been a sharp rise in bandhs in the city in recent times. All the political parties resort to the bandhs to express their views and this is totally counterproductive for the industries in the state. No one gains anything except the political conveners. There is a huge loss of manpower which translates into financial losses to the state exchequer. Mindless violence and destruction of public properties are rampant during the bandh. The daily earners are the worst hit as no income for them is tantamount to no food for the day. Medical patients also go through a harrowing time as it is difficult to get any timely medical assistance and in some cases, a bandh may become a life-threatening situation for them. In short, a bandh brings more misery to common people instead of solving any problem.

I appeal to the common people of the city to protest against the culture of bandhs and the unreasonable political decisions by the party in power. We must demonstrate our rights against this disruptive mode of the partisan politics which does not benefit the society at large.

Yours faithfully,

Devraj Singh
Kolkata

b. Letter Reporting Inaccuracy in a Newspaper Report

Sample:

Sender's Address Line
Date

Editor
The Modern Mirror
31, Eliot Road
Kolkata – 700056

Dear Editor,

There was an article published in your newspaper dated 17 April 2013, covering the 125th anniversary of Indian Model School. I find there are some factual errors in your report. First, the school celebrated its 150th anniversary and not its 125th, as has been reported by you. You also reported that it is run by foreign missionaries. It was established by a group of Indian missionaries in the year 1952. You also forgot to mention that the school has been a pioneer in modern education for the last 50 years. The Indian Modern School has also been running a separate section for downtrodden children which includes free education, books, uniforms and lunch.

Please rectify your mistake by printing a corrigendum.

Yours faithfully,

Ranjan Seth
Kolkata

c. Letter Reporting Lack of Civic Amenities in New Building Complex

Sample:

Sender's Address Line
Date

Editor
The Modern Mirror
31, Eliot Road
Kolkata – 700056

Dear Editor,

Our locality has been developed recently by a famous builder in association with the government housing department. The project was completed and the flats were handed over thereafter. The flat owners were assured of the basic civic facilities such as wide roads, electricity, water supply, markets and easy connectivity with the other parts of the city.

But the fact remains that none of the promises were fulfilled. The roads are incomplete even after one year. Thirty minutes of rain is enough to make the area waterlogged and the water takes 10 to 12 hours to drain out. Supply of water and electricity from the Kolkata Municipal Corporation are also very erratic. Frequent power cuts after sunset are causing a law and order problem. This makes commuting to and fro from office in the night most unsafe, especially for the young women in our neighbourhood. To add to this, there is a lack of public transport in the area and the promised connectivity is all a sham.

Are such big developers not accountable to the property owners once they have sold them the flats? Should we all continue being duped by these people who have convinced us to spend our life's savings in property in such areas of the city that are far from habitable?

I hope my letter has some effect in redressing our problems and bringing together others suffering a similar plight.

Thanking you,

Secretary
Residents' Association of Ruby Park Manor

d. Letter Reporting Cutting Down of Trees

Sample:

Sender's Address Line
Date

Editor
The Modern Mirror
31, Residency Road
Bangalore – 560031

Dear Editor

We, the residents of Whitefield, would like to voice our protest against the unnecessary destruction of trees in our locality. This is a major problem and contributes to the larger issue of the destruction of the green cover in our city. The municipality has decided to widen the road by 20 feet and as a result, they have been cutting down the old trees on both sides of the road. They propose to build a boulevard with seasonal flowering plants mainly to beautify the roads which does not justify destruction of 40 full-grown trees. It takes almost 15 years for a tree to reach maturity and some of these trees were over 30 years old. The road was a lovely shaded avenue and the proposed artificial beautification will not be able to restore its charm.

Trees maintain ecological balance and keep the environment clean. It is a shame that such activities in the name of development are destroying the very nature of our city and if we don't take heed, Bangalore, the city of gardens, will soon become the city of concrete.

Yours faithfully,

Mandira Shah

e. Letter Reporting Numerous Potholes on the Main Roads of the City

Sample:

Sender's Address Line
Date

Editor
The Morning Glory

225, Camac Street
Kolkata – 700 016

Dear Editor,

I would like to bring to the attention of the authorities the pitiful condition of the mains roads in the city. Several written complaints to the Public Works Department and the Kolkata Municipal Corporation have proved to be futile so as a last option, I am sending this letter to your newspaper with the hope that it will compel the authorities to do something.

The roads were in a terrible condition to begin with and after the onset of the monsoon it has became worse. The top layer has got washed away and with the onslaught of heavy traffic, there are potholes everywhere. As a result, everything moves really slowly, creating long traffic snarls, especially during the peak hours. It takes hours to travel even short distances and you cannot imagine the misery the common public has to face every day. Travelling on the city roads has become a nightmarish experience and the cost of maintaining vehicles has also gone up due to the extended commute and terrible roads.

We would like to know why a basic necessity like a proper road cannot be provided to the taxpayers, especially in a city that is supposedly built according to international standards. After the monsoon there will be temporary repair work which will last a very short time and then the whole process will be repeated next year. It is beyond my comprehension why the roads cannot be laid properly and citizens are not inconvenienced year after year.

I sincerely hope that media will pick up the issue and ultimately public opinion will force the authorities to take corrective measures.

Yours faithfully,

Raghav Sharma

To: editor@themorninggloryindia.com
Subject: Opinion on Large Number of Potholes in the City

Dear Editor,

I would like to bring to the attention of the authorities the pitiful condition of the mains roads in the city. Several written complaints to the Public Works Department and the Kolkata Municipal Corporation have proved to be futile so as a last option, I am sending this letter to your newspaper with the hope that it will compel the authorities to do something.

The roads were in a terrible condition to begin with and after the onset of the monsoon it has became worse. The top layer has got washed away and with the onslaught of heavy traffic, there are potholes everywhere. As a result, everything moves really slowly, creating long traffic snarls, especially during the peak hours. It takes hours to travel even short distances and you cannot imagine the misery the common public has to face every day. Travelling on the city roads has become a nightmarish experience and the cost of maintaining vehicles has also gone up due to the extended commute and terrible roads.

We would like to know why a basic necessity like a proper road cannot be provided to the taxpayers, especially in a city that is supposedly built according to international standards. After the monsoon there will be temporary repair work which will last a very short time and then the whole process will be repeated next year. It is beyond my comprehension why the roads cannot be laid properly and citizens are not inconvenienced year after year.

I sincerely hope that the media will pick up the issue and ultimately public opinion will force the authorities to take corrective measures.

Yours faithfully,

Raghav Sharma

Email Signature Line

f. Letter Reporting Unsafe Neighbourhood due to Lack of Street Lights

Sample:

Sender's Address Line
Date

Editor
The Morning Glory
225, Camac Street
Kolkata – 700 016

Dear Editor,

I live right on Garden View Road and I am writing to tell you how this area has become extremely unsafe post sunset and this is because there are no street lights on this entire stretch of road. This used to be a very respectable neigbourhood where working professionals, youngsters and kids would be seen walking about in the evenings. For the past month, all the streetlights have malfunctioned due to some electrical fault and the area has been plunged into darkness. As a result of this antisocial activities have increased in the area. Pickpockets and other thieves are having a free run. Residents of the area think twice before venturing out in the evenings and everyone needs to take a cab or drive even for short distances. The young women in our area have been teased by hooligans and also feel unsafe while coming home from schools, colleges and their offices unaccompanied by males.

Accidents have also become fairly common due to lack of street lights. Elderly people find it very difficult to walk even a short distance after dark. There have been many cases of people tripping and falling on the road fall resulting in injuries. Numerous complaints have been made to the concerned department of the Kolkata Municipal Corporation, but so far nothing has happened.

The Durga Puja festival is just around the corner. If the authorities fail to correct the situation before that, there will be a tremendous law and order problem during the festival nights. We are quite fed up and all our requests to the authorities have fallen on deaf ears. I hope this letter will have some effect and bring about some improvement in our situation.

Yours faithfully,

Narendra Jadeja

g. Letter Reporting Women's Safety Issues

Sample:

Sender's Address Line
Date

Editor
The Morning Glory
225, Camac Street
Kolkata – 700 016

Dear Editor,

In the aftermath of the Delhi Nirbhaya case, the country was up in arms and everyone was protesting violent crimes against women. Although this case garnered so much public opinion, the crux of the matter remains unresolved. The dark streets which proved to play a part in the gruesome case of Nirbhaya, plague our city as well. Stretches of Maidan and Park Street are every woman's nightmare post sundown. Young men on bikes and cars roam those streets like predators waiting to pounce on the women for fun. There have been quite a few reported incidents in recent times where young and middle-aged women alike, have been chased by bike gangs and in two instances even been picked up by a group of boys in a car.

Dark stretches of road and the lack of police patrols in this area have made matters worse and if things don't improve, we could very well have a Nirbhaya case in our own city. We are afraid for our daughters, sisters and mothers every time they travel to these areas.

I hope this letter works as a wake-up call to the authorities and they take steps towards preventing such crimes against women.

Yours faithfully,

Naina Singh

h. Letter Reporting Wrong Dates in an Obituary

Sample:

Sender's Address Line
Date

Editor
The Morning Glory
225, Camac Street
Kolkata – 700 016

Dear Editor,

The morning edition of your paper dated 23 September, carried an obituary of my father, the ex-governor of the city, late Shri Surinder Rana. We regret to point out that dates were all mixed up. He expired on 23 September 2013 and the memorial service was to be held on 25 September 2013 at 4.30 p.m. at the Town Hall. The published dates in your newspaper were

22 September as the day of death and 23 September as the date for the memorial ceremony.

This wrong information has created endless confusion and caused lot of inconvenience to the bereaved family.

We would request you to publish the obituary again with the correct dates at no extra cost to us in tomorrow's edition, so that people are informed, and they can arrive at the venue to pay their last respects to my father.

Thanking you

Viren Rana

2. SCHOOL LETTERS

These are very important letters exchanged between parents, teachers, school principals and other authorities regarding behaviour, performances, requests and complaints. The letters should be polite, brief and keep the affairs of the student in question foremost.

Since these letters are of great importance with respect to both the child and the institution, they must be drafted with care. Request letters and leave letters must clearly mention dates and timings to ensure that there is no confusion. In some cases the telephone number should also be mentioned to allow parents and teachers to communicate directly and fix up meetings at their convenience.

a. Letter from Teacher to a Parent regarding a Student's Performance

Letters from teachers to parents should be written with a positive view. The basic reason of writing this letter is not to complain for underperformance but to display concern for the student.

Sample:

Manohar Prasad
Class Teacher – XIB
Modern Boys School
32, Andrewsgunj
New Delhi – 110034
Date

Mr Anup Kothari
44, Lajpat Nagar
New Delhi – 110 024

Dear Sir,

Your son, Anish Kothari has always been a very consistent student and has performed brilliantly in all his unit tests. He is very focused and has got a positive attitude towards studies and shows equal interest in other extracurricular activities.

However, in recent weeks, we have observed that he looks distracted and out of focus. As a result his grades are going down. He looks depressed and disinterested in everything around him. As his class teacher, I am quite concerned about him and will need your help to find out the root cause of the problem.

Would it possible for you to come to school on Saturday, 12 May 2013, at 11.30 a.m.? If the timing is not convenient for you, please call me at 98399 40080 and we can fix up an alternate time. Please treat this as urgent as we all want your son to bounce back on his feet and continue his performance as before.

Thanking you,

Signature

Manohar Prasad

b. Letter from Teacher to Parent regarding Drug Consumption by a Student

Sample:

Raghav Trivedi
Class Teacher – XIIA

Model Public School
11 Barakhamba Road
New Delhi – 110004
Date

Mr Nilesh Vardhan
Flat No 3A
Godavari Apartments
Saket
New Delhi – 110 017

Dear Sir,

Your son, Ankit Vardhan, a student of class XII A has been caught smoking marijuana cigarettes in school. Not only is consumption of any kind of drug illegal, it is also a gross violation of school codes. Since this is a very serious breach of conduct and could even result in expulsion, we would like to discuss the matter with you before we take any disciplinary action on our side.

We believe that the student's well-being is the most important thing in our school. This is also an extremely crucial period for Ankit as it is the final year of school. Any harsh action might spoil his future career, but it is also equally important to restrain him and make him understand that drugs will ruin his life. His participation is most crucial.

You are requested to meet the Principal at the conference room on the first floor on Saturday, 26 May 2013, at 11.30 a.m. to further discuss the matter.

Warm regards,

Signature

Raghav Trivedi

c. Letter from School Principal Suspending Student for Disruptive Behaviour

Sample:

Prem Chand Singh
Class Teacher – XC
Golden Horizon School

23, Block D
Saket
New Delhi – 110017
Date

Mr T.N. Verma
32, Lajpat Nagar
New Delhi – 110 024

Dear Sir,

We regret to inform you that your son Rishi Verma, a student of Class XC, has been suspended for 10 days from school with immediate effect (23 May). This extreme step was unavoidable and is a consequence of his violent behaviour in the lunch room yesterday. He punched one boy and made his nose bleed and pushed two others against a wall. He also damaged some school property during the scuffle. When he was ordered by the teacher to leave the lunch room, he disobeyed him and continued creating a ruckus. It is only with the Principal's intervention that things became manageable.

It has been observed that Ankit's volatile temper and intolerance towards other students are causing problems for others in the class. He is distracting the whole class. He has been verbally warned on a number of occasions but without any effect.

The suspension comes as the final warning. If he does not mend his ways, we will have no other choice but to rusticate him from our school as the last resort. We sincerely hope that the situation will be sorted out with counselling and parental guidance and we will not be forced to take this extreme step.

We need your cooperation.

Yours faithfully,

Signature

Prem Chand Singh

d. Letter to Principal regarding Child's Suspension

Letters written to Principals have to be formal, short and polite. The purpose of the letter should be specific and relevant. If there is a serious problem concerning the student, the Principal's advice should be sought to solve the problem through discussions. Concern and well-being of the child should be highlighted in the letter and the details of the child should be clearly mentioned. Also mention your contact details clearly so that the school can get in touch with you if required.

Sample:

Sender's Address Line
Phone number/email address
Date

Mr K. Mathur
Principal
New Dimension School
12, Ballygunge Circular Road,
Kolkata – 700 019

Dear Sir,

My son, Aneek Saluja, is a student of Class XA of your school. He has been suspended for a week with effect from 6 February 2013 due to habituated neglect of his studies and disturbing the class.

I understand that the school suspends students as the last resort and although it is the most difficult situation for parents to handle, I can understand that the situation would have forced you to make such a decision. I would be grateful if you could please let me know a time that is convenient for you so that I might come in to meet you and discuss my son's problems. I will need your guidance in helping him back to his feet as he used to be a star student up until last year. Suddenly, his behaviour and attitude have changed and I am unable to understand the reason for this dramatic transformation. Any advice from your end would be most welcome.

I look forward to an early reply.

Thanking you,

Signature

Aveek Saluja

e. Letter from Parent to Teacher regarding Child's Performance

Sample:

Sender's Address Line
Phone number/email address
Date

Mrs Chanda Kumar
Class Teacher – XA
Ruby International School
20, Survey Park
Kolkata – 700 056

Madam,

My son, Adil Mehra, is a student of your class. I find that over the last few months his grades in the unit tests are steadily declining and this is a matter of great concern for us as Adil has always been a good and consistent performer.

I would request you to spare a few minutes at your convenience to discuss the problems Adil is having in following the lessons and whether he needs to join the special tutorial classes after school to improve his grades. Your evaluation of the whole situation is of great importance to me. I am certain that with your valuable advice we will be able to guide Adil in the right direction.

Thanking you for your attention.

Yours faithfully,

Signature

Uday Mehra

To: chanda.kumar@gmail.com
Subject: Regarding Adil Mehra's Academic Performance

Madam,

My son, Adil Mehra, is a student of your class. I find that over the last few months his grades in the unit tests are steadily declining and this is a matter of great concern for us as Adil has always been a good and consistent performer.

I would request you to spare a few minutes at your convenience to discuss the problems Adil is having in following the lessons and whether he needs to join the special tutorial classes after school to improve his grades. Your evaluation of the whole situation is of great importance to me. I am certain that with your valuable advice we will be able to guide Adil in the right direction.

Thanking you for your attention.

Yours faithfully,

Uday Mehra

Email Signature Line

f. Parent to Teacher regarding Child's Misbehaviour

Sample:

Sender's Address Line
Phone Number/Email Address
Date

Mrs Dina Pathak
Class Teacher – XA
Ruby International School
34 Ruby Park
Kolkata – 700065

Dear Madam,

I am writing this letter in response to your letter dated 29 January 2013, regarding my son Rehan Kaul's recent misbehavior in the class. As requested by you I will be in school to meet you at 2 p.m. on 9 February 2013, for a discussion.

I would appreciate it if you could share with me the exact incident that Rehan was involved in and under what circumstances it happened. I strongly feel that children need to learn to be responsible for their actions and there is no excuse for bad manners.

I need your advice to rectify the situation and help him develop good manners. My primary concern is to make him realize that this kind of behaviour is unacceptable and there should not be any recurrence of the same in the future.

I would appreciate your prompt reply and look forward to a fruitful meeting with you.

Yours faithfully,

Signature

Randhir Kaul

g. Apology Letter from a Student

This kind of letter should be polite and does not require the sender's address line or signature as it is primarily an interaction between the student and the teacher.

Sample:

Mrs M. Francis
Class Teacher – XIIB
Model Public School
11 Barakhamba Road
New Delhi – 110004
Date

Respected Madam,

I sincerely apologize for my behavior in class on 5 February. My actions were regrettable and I assure you that I will never repeat them under any circumstances no matter what the provocation. From now onwards, I will be respectful to you and be attentive to all your instructions.

I have realized my mistake and will make sure that I concentrate only on my studies and strive to be a good student in its true meaning.

I hope you accept my apology.

Yours faithfully,

Vikram Pandey
Roll no 24
Class XIIB

h. Request Letter

Sample:

Sender's Address Line

Phone Number/Email Address
Date

Mrs Maria Lobo
Principal
Green View School

Madam,

My son, Avik Singh, is a student of Class XA of your school and he has been studying in this school for the last 10 years. He has always been an above-average student but now I find he needs a little extra help in his studies as his grades are going down and he cannot cope with the lessons in class. I think he cannot manage without extra tuitions. At home, both me and my husband are busy professionals and cannot help him much. We feel that he is in need of professional guidance.

Under the circumstances, I would request you to arrange for some extra tutorial lessons after school hours. I know that there are extra classes after school for some of the senior boys and I would be very grateful if Avik could join the group as well.

Thanking you,

Signature

Anita Singh

i. Sick Leave Letter

Sample:

Sender's Address Line
Phone Number/Email Address
Date

Mr A.P. Chowdhury
Class Teacher, XA
New Model School
102, Loudon Street
Kolkata – 700 017

Dear Sir,

My son, Abhishek Mehta, a student of your class, has been suffering from viral fever since 4 February 2013. He has been advised bed rest for seven days by our family doctor and therefore he will be unable to attend his classes till 11 February 2013.

I would request you to excuse Abhishek's absence from school for one week.

I would request you to give him some assignments which he can work on when he is little better. This will help him to rejoin classes with ease and pick up from where he had left.

Thanking you,

Signature

Ajit Mehta

j. Admission Letter

Sample:

Sender's Address Line
Date

Mr B.B. Kalra
Principal (Junior School)
Horizon Day School

Dear Sir,

I would like to apply for my daughter's admission in Class I in your esteemed school for the session starting in April 2013. Your school is renowned for academics, discipline, as well as extra-curricular activities.

My daughter Rachna Rai has completed her nursery school from Springtime Tiny Tots in Mumbai. She has been doing quite well and she takes a keen interest in other activities in her school and also has a keen interest in art. Now that she has completed her nursery schooling, she needs to join a reputed institution like yours where she will learn and grow under your able guidance.

I am aware of the fact that admission in your school is highly competitive and merit is the only criteria for getting in. I hereby submit my daughter's application along with the required documents for your perusal.

Looking forward to a positive reply.

Thanking you,

Signature

Kiran Rai

k. Transfer Letter

Sample:

Sender's Address Line
Date

The Principal
Maria International School
25, Barakhamba Road
New Delhi – 110 001

Dear Sir,

Arnav Saxena, Roll No 12
Student of Class VIIIA

I am an officer with the Indian Armed Forces and my son, Arnav Saxena, a student of Class VIIIA, has been studying in your school for the last eight years. Under the school's able guidance, he has so far, performed very well in his class. The ambience and the cordial relationship between teachers and students make your school very special.

Unfortunately, Arnav has to leave the school in the new session starting from April 2013, as I have been recently been transferred to the Eastern Command Headquarters in Kolkata and am supposed to join my duties next month. My family will follow at the end of Arnav's academic year.

I would, therefore, request you to issue a transfer certificate to my son along with a copy of his report card so that I can start his admission process in Kolkata.

We sincerely regret the fact Arnav will miss out the opportunity to continue studying under your tutelage and we thank you for your contribution to his academic life.

I look forward to an early response.

Yours faithfully,

Signature

Colonel Abhay Saxena

I. Request for Leave

Sample:

Sender's Address Line
Date

Mrs Anila Mehta
Class Teacher – XB
Maria International School
22, Dabolim
Goa – 403801

Madam,

I would be grateful if you please allow my daughter, Smita Yadav, a student of your class, to be given four days of special leave. This leave is due to an unavoidable family function in Bangalore that we all have to attend and Smita will obviously have to accompany us.

The dates of the function are from 24 February to 27 February 2013 (both days inclusive) and I hope you will excuse her absence for those days. I would earnestly request you to please give her homework for the next 4 days so that on her return she will be able to catch up to some extent.

I am aware of the school's strict policy regarding special leave during term, but this is an exceptional situation where her presence is essential. I regret that she will miss her classes but she will work hard and complete all pending assignments upon her return.

I hope you will understand.

Yours faithfully,

Signature

Y.S. Yadav

3. LETTERS TO THE GOVERNMENT

These letters must clearly mention dates and facts and be brief as government representatives are unlikely to go beyond the basic facts of a case.

a. Letter about Non-Receipt of Voter's ID Card

Sample:

Sender's Address Line
Date

Election Commission of India (West Bengal)
32, Gopal Modi Road
Kolkata – 700 031

Dear Sir,

Non-Receipt of Voter's ID Card

I had applied for my Voter's ID Card in the Form 6 and sent it along with the address proof and all other documents as prescribed therein on 24 September 2012. I was called for photographs in the local municipality office in January 2013. I have got a photocopy and a receipt for the same. I regret to inform you that till date I have not received my Voter's ID Card.

I have enquired several times at your office but have got the same reply each time. The officials keep saying that it has been dispatched and will be delivered to my address shortly. In spite of the repeated assurance from your department, the ID has not reached me so far.

On 11 August 2013, when I visited your office, I was informed that my ID Card could not be sent due to non-availability of photographs. I immediately went back to the municipality office dealing with the Voter's ID Card and got new photographs taken which were then submitted again. I would like to know the present status of my ID Card. I am enclosing photocopies of all the documents submitted initially for your ready reference.

I would request you to please look into the matter and please arrange to send my Voter's ID Card as early as possible.

Thanking you,

Signature

Raghu Raj

b. Letter Complaining about Wrong Name on Voter's ID Card

Sample:

Sender's Address Line
Date

Election Commission of India (West Bengal)
32, Gopal Modi Road
Kolkata – 700 031

Dear Sir,

Wrong name on Voter's ID Card

I had applied for a Voter's ID Card in March 2012. Subsequently, I was called for photographs in August 2012, in the local municipal office on 22, Sarat Bose Road.

I received my Voter's ID Card issued by your office in June 2013. On scrutiny of my card I realized that my name has been printed wrongly on it. It should have been Raman Kher instead of Raghav Kher.

I immediately went back to your office to report the matter and get the mistake rectified. I resubmitted all the documents along with the wrong Voter's ID Card. I was assured that a new card with my correct name would reach me in a month's time.

More than three months have passed and I am yet to receive my Voter's ID Card. The elections are going to be held in two months' time and without the Voter's ID Card I will not be qualified to vote. Under the circumstances, I would request you to please instruct your department to issue my card immediately.

Thanking you,

Signature

Raman Kher

c. Letter about Non-Receipt of Adhar Card

Sample:

Sender's Address Line
Date

Unique Identification of India
Government of India
Planning Commission
3rd Floor, Tower II
Jeevan Bharti Building
New Delhi – 110 001

Dear Sir,

Non-Receipt of Adhar Card

I had enrolled for the Adhar Card in December 2012 and my Enrolment No is 0000/999/3355114 dated 13 December 2012. I have not received my Adhar Card so far. On enquiry I was advised to check the delivery status online.

I checked online on 13 September 2013 and it said that my card had been delivered on 21 September 2013. Since I have not received the Adhar Card yet, I enquired again at your office and was told to find out the latest update from the nearest post office. The Sarat Bose Road Post Office informed me that they have not dispatched any Adhar Card to my address.

The Government of India intends to launch direct subsidy transfer to the bank account of Adhar Card holders for the subsidized gas cylinders from December 2013. Subsidized gas cylinders will be supplied only to the customers with Adhar Card numbers through their bank accounts. To avail of this facility, I need my Adhar Card immediately.

Please help me to get my card without any further delay.

Thanking you,

Signature

Anurag Ramani

4. COLLEGE LETTERS

College letters are of three kinds. The first variety is written at the pre-college stage enquiring about courses, scholarships, hostel accommodation and admission processes. The second variety is written while in college or even after passing out from college, enquiring about marksheets, recovery of deposits, degrees, attested documents and other administration-related work. There is a third kind of college letter which is the reference letter written by, or requested from professors and mentors in the department that the sender belongs to.

a. Request for College Transcript

Sample:

Sender's Address Line
Date

Registrar's Office
St Andrews College
78, Green Park
New Delhi – 110015

Dear Sir,

My name is Gopinath Mishra and I was a student of your college (2009–2012). I graduated with a first class in BA History (Hons) in 2012.

I would like to request you to please arrange for a copy of my third-year transcript and the original BA Degree which is mandatory for admission to postgraduate courses in India and abroad.

I would be grateful if you please let me know when the transcripts will be available so that I can come personally to the college office and collect it. The transcript request form, duly filled in, is submitted herewith.

Looking forward to a prompt response from your side.

Yours faithfully,

Signature

Gopinath Mishra

b. Request for Letter of Recommendation

Sample:

Sender's Address Line
Date

Dr Atish Raghavan
Head of Department (English)
Salt Lake University
Sector – 1C
Salt Lake

Dear Dr Raghavan,

I am writing this letter to request you for a letter of recommendation for me. My name is Surbhi Singh and I was a student of your MA (English) Class from 2010 to 2012. I took your Victorian Literature and Modern American Poetry courses and finished with a high first division in both papers.

I am in the process of applying for admission in the PHD Programme in English at the Univeristy of Texas (Austin) and a recommendation letter from the university I had last attended is required. I was hoping that you might be able to write me a letter of recommendation since you taught me and were familiar with my work. I am going to do my PHD on Victorian Studies and my area of focus will be the philosophy of consumption in this period.

Along with all the necessary documents, marksheets and other information you may need to write the recommendation, I am also attaching the paper that I had presented in my second year for your course on the 'Symbolism of Food in Victorian Novels'.

A few of the other essays that I wrote for your classes are also enclosed for your ready reference.

If you need any more information, please contact me on my cell phone. My number is 2233446688. I have also enclosed one self-addressed envelope for your convenience.

Thank you for your time and consideration.

Yours faithfully,

Signature

Surbhi Singh

c. Letter of Thanks for a Job Reference

Sample:

Sender's Address Line
Date

Mr Manoj Sahai
General Manager (HRD)
Universal Lights Corporation
25, Santacruz Central
Mumbai – 400 054

Dear Sir,

Thank you for the reference letter you wrote to my prospective employers, Green Valley Limited. Your excellent reference on my training and my tenure under you has helped a great deal in my being selected for the job. You will be happy to note that I have received my appointment letter for the new job. Your recommendation was highly valued and it made a great impression on my current employer.

Thanking you once again for your generous assistance.

Yours faithfully,

Signature

Manohar Apte

d. Letter of Thanks for an Academic Award

Sender's Address Line
Date

The Principal
St Andrews College
32, Colbert Lane
Dublin
Ireland

Dear Sir,

I am writing this letter to express my sincere thanks to your office for selecting me as the recipient of the 'Student of the Year' award.

This award is a great inspiration to me and will make a great difference to my performance and self esteem. As you know I am here on a merit-based scholarship that takes care of my tuition fees. This additional scholarship will be more than adequate to take care of my living expenses and give me more time to concentrate on my academics. This award will make me and my family proud and will continue to inspire me to reach greater heights and successes.

I am grateful for your confidence in me and I will aspire to keep the faith that you bestowed upon me.

Thank you once again.

Yours faithfully,

Signature

Raman Rajpal
International Student's Union President

e. Enquiry about External Corporate Scholarship for Meritorious Students

Sender's Address Line
Phone number/email address
Date

General Manager (Administration)
Modern Steel Corporation
22, Industrial Estate
New Linking Road
Andheri West
Mumbai – 400 022

Dear Sir,

I would be grateful if you please furnish the necessary information about the scholarships under your EXCEL programme earmarked for meritorious students applying to foreign universities for postgraduate courses.

My name is Ankit Kumar and I have just completed my BA in Economics (Hons) from Christian College, Mumbai and have secured 75% in Economics. I would like to do my postgraduation in the same field and have applied to King's College, London and London School of Economics for an MA program in Economics. I have received conditional offer letters from both universities and can start this fall if my financial requirements are fulfilled. I would be grateful if you take a look at my case and consider me for your esteemed scholarship.

A copy of my application and offer letter is enclosed along with my transcripts, bank statements and a recommendation letter.

If you require any further information, please send me an email or call me on 22553 44299.

Looking forward to a favourable reply

Yours faithfully,

Signature

Ankit Kumar

f. Refusal to Write Letter of Recommendation

Sender's Address Line
Phone number/email address
Date

Mr Lakhsman Kedia
45, Janpath Marg
New Delhi 110 011

Dear Lakshman,

I have received your letter dated 23 September 2013, requesting me to write a recommendation letter required for your higher studies. As far as I remember you were not part of any of my projects or my special classes. I am not familiar with your abilities, strong points and accomplishments which should be significantly highlighted in a recommendation letter.

I will be honest and admit that I am not the right person to write a recommendation for you. Based on my knowledge of you I could at best write a neutral letter which would be of no use to you.

I am sorry that I cannot be of help to you and I wish you success in your future.

Yours sincerely,

Professor Jagdeep Singh

g. Acceptance of Admission Letter

Sender's Address Line
Phone number/email address
Date

Director of Admission
Irish Church College
325, Andheri East
Mumbai – 400 021

Dear Sir,

I have been offered admission in your esteemed college vide letter dated 29 September 2013 to the MA programme in Economics (Hons) for 2013–16 session. I accept the offer of admission with the rules and regulations mentioned therein.

I enclose a demand draft for ₹ 20,000 dated 4 October 2013, drawn in favour of the Irish Church College towards admission and fees for the first year.

I am looking forward to joining the course in this esteemed institution.

Thank you very much for selecting me.

Yours faithfully,

Gopal Kumar

h. Enquiry about Scholarship

Sender's Address Line
Phone number/email address
Date

The Registrar
Jodhpur Engineering College
Nehru Nagar
Residency Road
Jodhpur – 340033
Rajasthan

Dear Sir,

I have been offered admission in the Department of Chemical Engineering in your college for the session 2013–17. I have already sent my acceptance letter along with the bank draft as required in the admission letter.

The purpose of this letter is to enquire about scholarships available to graduate-level students who have secured 95% and above in their school-leaving examinations.

I have obtained 97% in my ISC from Jaipur Public School and I also placed second in the JEE for engineering.

I would be obliged if you could please provide me with the information about any financial assistance available for the graduate-level students for the current academic year, availability of application forms and the last date of application.

I come from a weak financial background and any scholarship will help reduce the financial burden on my family.

Thanking you for your time and consideration.

Yours faithfully,

Signature

Rupchand Ghelot

i. Deferral of Admission Letter

Sender's Address Line
Phone number/email address
Date

The Registrar
Management Institute of Mumbai
25, Andheri (East)
Mumbai – 400 050

Dear Sir,

This has reference to the admission letter from the Management Institute of Mumbai, dated 25 September 2013, for the PGDM course in Management Studies for the session 2013–15.

I would be greatly obliged if you could allow me to defer my admission by one year due to financial constraints. I had applied for an education loan from the bank and it was approved. But in the meantime, as per a Reserve

Bank directive, all education loans have been deferred by three months. My bank has assured me that they will start payment of my approved education loan from January 2014. Due to non-availability of finance options, I will not be able to pay my fees for the first year within the due date.

I would request you to please consider my case and allow me deferral by one year. I am looking forward to joining your prestigious institute next year.

Thanking you for your consideration.

Yours faithfully,

Signature

Manoj Solkar

To: admissions@mim.ac.in
Subject: Request for Deferral of Admission

Dear Sir,

This has reference to the admission letter from the Management Institute of Mumbai, dated 25 September 2013, for the PGDM course in Management Studies for the session 2013–15.

I would be greatly obliged if you could allow me to defer my admission by one year due to financial constraints. I had applied for an education loan from the bank and it was approved. But in the meantime, as per a Reserve Bank directive, all education loans have been deferred by three months. My bank has assured me that they will start payment of my approved education loan from January 2014. Due to non-availability of finance options, I will not be able to pay my fees for the first year within the due date.

I would request you to please consider my case and allow me deferral by one year. I am looking forward to joining your prestigious institute next year.

Thanking you for your consideration.

Yours faithfully,

Manoj Solkar

Email Signature Line

j. Appeal Letter to Reconsider Rejected Application

Sender's Address Line
Phone number/email address
Date

The Principal
Greenwood College
35, National Highway
Shimla
Himachal Pradesh

Sir,

I had applied for a BA in Sociology for the session 2013–16 in your college as this has the best sociology department in the country. The cut-off mark required for admission this year was 86%. I have secured 85% in my school-leaving examination.

I was genuinely disappointed to receive a rejection letter from the college though my score was just below the cut-off. I was suffering from chicken pox during the final examination so I could not do justice to the examinations. But it does not reflect my true ability and accomplishment in studies. My marks in the Selection Tests conducted by school were around 95%. I attach herewith certified copies of my medical certificate and the original mark sheets of the Selection Tests for your scrutiny.

I sincerely hope that you will please reconsider my case and give me an opportunity to study in your renowned college.

Looking forward to hearing from you

Thanking you

Signature

Ranjana Bansal

5. ENQUIRY LETTERS

These are formal letters enquiring about a specific product or service. It deals with specific information required for different purposes. The intention of the letter should be clear and direct so that the recipient can respond accordingly.

a. Enquiry about a New Product

Sender's Address Line
Phone number/email address
Date

Mr Archan Bhandari
Marketing Manager
Household Consumer Goods
Brilliant Gadgets
22, New Road
Mumbai – 400 001

Dear Sir,

Enquiry about the New Catalogue

You have launched an extensive range of new electronic products in the market. I would like to know whether they are available all over India in your showrooms, or can customers buy them only in Maharashtra? In the advertisement published in the *Times of India,* you have not mentioned a price range for any of the items. I request you to please send me a catalogue giving the technical specifications and prices. It will help me to pinpoint the exact items I intend to buy for my home.

Please also notify me if there is any discount scheme on these items.

Your prompt action will be highly appreciated.

Thanking you,

Signature

Vinesh Varghav

b. Enquiry about a Course

Company Letterhead

Date

The Director
Management Skills Training Centre
4th Floor
35, Church Street
Mumbai – 400 035

Dear Sir,

Short Term Courses for Middle Management

We would request you to provide us with the detailed information about the Human Resource Development Programme for mid-level executives.

Our company is a manufacturing unit and hence deals with a large number of workers both skilled and unskilled. There are lots of sensitive issues between the management and workers that need to be dealt with in a diplomatic manner. Keeping this in mind, we need a customized course that will help our managers to deal with the matters related above.

We will send a batch of 10 officers and would appreciate it if the classes are conducted after working hours (6 p.m. onwards on weekdays and on Saturdays from 9 a.m.). This arrangement will not disturb our day-to-day functions.

Could you please let us know about the fees for the course and whether we are eligible for any discount.

Looking forward to an early response.

Thanking you,

Signature

Ramesh Meena
General Manager HRD

PART II

Personal Letters

The Basic Format of a Personal Letter

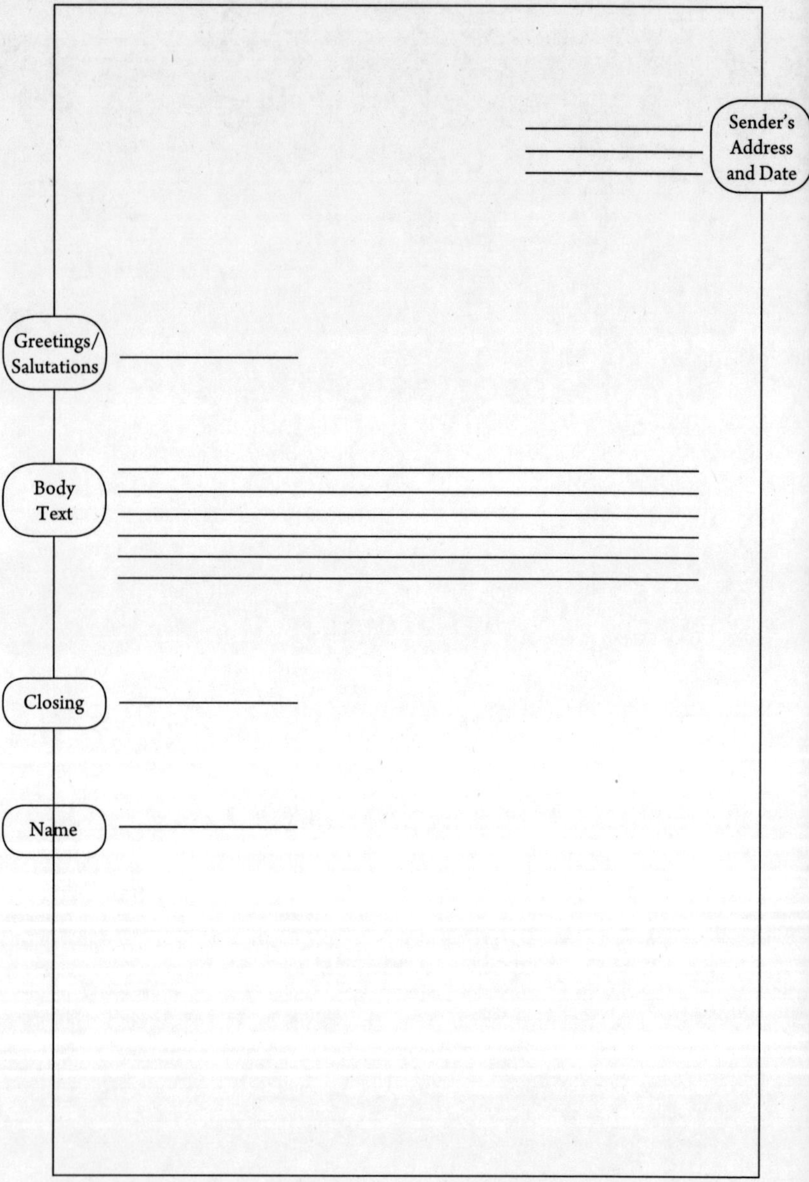

Types of Personal Letters

These letters are an informal exchange of communication between friends, relatives and well-acquainted people. These letters are sent to convey a personalized message to near and dear ones and it shows that the concerned person is in your thoughts and it is often a much appreciated gesture. A few lines written with sincere feelings make a big difference especially during celebrations and mourning periods. The object of writing letters during such times is to share your thoughts as well as reach out to your near and dear ones during good or bad times.

A thoughtfully handwritten letter carries much more value than an email during certain occasions.

Apart from these kind of letters, there are also those letters that are written to neighbours, acquaintances, landlords, tenants and other social contacts in order to dispense information, make complaints and send out greetings.

Personal letters are of two types: social and intimate. The nature of the letter is determined by the relationship between the sender and the addressee. Close friends and families share an intimate relationship so all formalities like the address line, traditional greetings and closings can be dispensed with, whereas letters to other social contacts can maintain a certain formal approach and structure.

1. BIRTHDAY LETTERS

a. Birthday Letter to a Family Friend

Sample:

Sender's Address Line
Date

Dear Bob,

Wish you all the very best on this special day. We pray that all your dreams come true and the year is filled with happiness, good health and success.

Birthday wishes are not meant to remind you that you have become a year older, but of your happy existence in this world.

Have a great time and enjoy yourself.

Once again a very happy birthday to you from all of us.

Best wishes,

Sandra and John Smith

b. Birthday Letter to a Child

Sample:

Date

Dear Jojo,

Today is your special day. You are turning seven. Another year older! Each day of our lives, we are grateful that you were born to us. You are a wonderful child and we wanted you to know that as today is your very special day. We will always wish and pray that all the special things that mean most to you come true.

Keep smiling and have 365 days of fun.

A very happy birthday.

With love,

Mum and Dad

c. Birthday Letter for a Milestone Birthday (18, 21, 30, 40, 50, 60 and each decade thereafter)

Sample:

Sender's Address Line
Date

Dear Karuna,

Welcome to the 60s club. Now that you have become a senior citizen, you can avail of all the wonderful benefits that our country has for our kind.

Always remember age is just a number and now you have only 40 years to be a century old.

You have enriched our lives with your warmth and joy. You are an amazing and absolutely gorgeous 60-year-old.

Here's wishing you a great 60th birthday and a wonderful time for the next decade.

Best wishes,

Nina

d. Birthday Letter to a Spouse

Sample:

Date

Dear Rahul,

On this day, I would like to thank you for being your wonderful self and also let you know that you mean so much to me.

I wish you love, wisdom and strength on this special day. May the years ahead be as glorious as those that have past.

Wish you a very happy birthday.

With all my love,

Diya

To: rahulroy79@gmail.com
Subject: Happy Birthday

Dear Rahul,

On this day, I would like to thank you for being your wonderful self and also let you know that you mean so much to me.

I wish you love, wisdom and strength on this special day. May the years ahead be as glorious as those that have past.

Wish you a very happy birthday.

With all my love,

Diya

e. Birthday Letter to a Parent

Sample:

Date

Dear Dad,

I want to let you know how I appreciate everything that you have done for me and how you have always been my very own rock of support and friendship. You were there for me during the toughest periods of my life and I just want to say thank you and hope that today is a wonderful day for you.

Welcome to the 50s, Dad and I hope that this is only a halfway mark for all the wonderful times ahead.

With love,

Sanjana

2. LETTERS FOR SPECIAL OCCASIONS

Special days are celebrated to express love and appreciation for your loved ones. We remember our parents' love and affection by making special efforts on Mother's Day and Father's Day. Other special days are Children's Day, Teacher's Day, Friendship Day and Women's Day. These should be personal handwritten letters showing that these special people are in your thoughts.

a. Mother's Day Letter

Sample:

Date

Dearest Mum,

You have always been a wonderful mother and I am truly blessed to have you as my guide, support and friend. Your love and prayers have kept me safe and strong. You have taught me the true values of life and always been a pillar of strength for me. You are my inspiration.

Thank you for being my mother; you are truly God's gift to me.

Here's wishing you a very Happy Mother's Day.

With love,

Your daughter

To: chandanakohli@gmail.com
Subject: Happy Mother's Day

Dearest Mum,

You have always been a wonderful mother and I am truly blessed to have you as my guide, support and friend. Your love and prayers have kept me safe and strong. You have taught me the true values of life and always been a pillar of strength for me. You are my inspiration.

Thank you for being my mother; you are truly God's gift to me.

Here's wishing you a very Happy Mother's Day.

With love,

Your daughter

b. Father's Day Letter

Sample:

Date

Dearest Dad,

Today is Father's Day – a day to appreciate and honour fathers all over the world. I consider myself lucky to have you as my father. You made my childhood days delightful and full of fun.

I still cherish the principles you taught me in life and practice it always. You made me realize the meaning of courage and the importance of a good and purposeful life. You have been always my source of inspiration and my all-time hero. Your spirit and love has always brightened my life.

Thank you for being my Dad and wish you a very happy Father's Day

Lots of love,

Siri

c. Children's Day Letter

Sample:

Date

Dear Class VB,

Today is Children's Day and it is time for fun and cheer. You are the future of our country and the next generation of mankind. May your lives be good and prosperous and may the fun and laughter always be with you.

Reach for the sky and scale new heights. I wish you a bright and cheerful tomorrow and always.

Best wishes,

Mrs Ratnamani

d. Teachers' Day Letter

Sample:

Date

Dear Mrs Singh,

Thank you for being such an outstanding teacher. You always motivated us to do well in our studies and at the same time encouraged us to participate in all kinds of extra-curricular activities. Your patience and enthusiasm have helped us understand the true meaning of education.

Thank you for being a mentor of our heart and souls and wish you a very happy Teacher's Day.

Warm wishes,

Class XB

e. Friendship Day Letter

Sample:

Date

Dear Stuti,

Happy Friendship Day. I want to thank you for being such a wonderful friend. I will always remember that you have been by my side during my hour of need as well as during the good times. You have made me realize the meaning of a true friend.

I hope our friendship grows stronger with every passing day. I appreciate everything you do and you are the one person who knows how to cheer me up even on the dullest day. My life would be empty and lonely without your friendship.

I wish you great happiness and may all your dreams come true.

With lots of love,

Shaina

f. Women's Day Letter

International Women's Day falls on 8 March every year. This day marks the celebration of womanhood. These letters could be sent to one's women friends, sisters, or even wives in order to make them feel special.

Sample:

Date

Dear Shalini,

Happy Women's Day. Today, I would like express my appreciation of your love and compassion which has made my life happy and complete.

Not only are women mothers, wives and daughters, they are also the best things about our world and make our lives worthwhile. A life without your presence would have been barren. You add meaning to our existence and bring us a world of happiness. Women are a perfect blend of strength, courage and love and you are my personal living embodiment of all that is wonderful about women.

All my best wishes,

Your husband

3. INVITATION LETTERS

Invitation letters are more cordial and more personal than invitation cards. These letters are specially written to close family and friends as prior intimation of the oncoming celebration before the formal invitation cards follow. These letters should mention the following:

- Date and time
- Venue
- If an RSVP is required
- The occasion

a. Wedding Invitation from Parents of the Bride/Groom

Sample:

Sender's Address Line
Date

Dear Sunita and Dev,

We are happy to inform you that our daughter Ishika is going to be a bride. She is getting married to her long-time sweetheart, Rishav, in Delhi on 9 October 2012, at the Coronation Hall at Vasant Kunj. The complete address along with date and time of functions are given in the enclosed invitation card. It would be our great pleasure if you and your family join us on this happy occasion.

We are looking forward to seeing you. Please do let us know your plans by 30 Sept 2012.

Best wishes,

Ranjit and Maya

To: devpatel@gmail.com
Subject: Wedding Invitation

Dear Sunita and Dev,

We are happy to inform you that our daughter Ishika is going to be a bride. She is getting married to her long-time sweetheart, Rishav, in Delhi on 9

October 2012, at the Coronation Hall at Vasant Kunj. The complete address along with date and time of functions are given in the invitation card which will reach you mail. It would be our great pleasure if you and your family join us on this happy occasion.

We are looking forward to seeing you. Please do let us know your plans by 30 Sept 2012.

Best wishes,

Ranjit and Maya

b. Wedding Invitation from Divorced Parents of the Bride/Groom

Sample:

Sender's Address Line
Date

Dear Mr Bhalla,

Neeta Singh and Ram Acharyya have great pleasure to announce the marriage of their daughter Rimi on 15 October 2012, at the Blue Diamond Hotel Banquet Hall at 7 p.m. You are cordially invited to join them and make the celebration a great success.

They look forward to seeing you and your family on this special occasion.

The invitation card with detailed programme and address will reach you shortly.

Best wishes,

Neeta Singh

c. Invitation from the Remarried Mother of the Groom

Sample:

Sender's Address Line
Date

Dear Rohit,

Mrs Rachna Mehra and Virender Singh are delighted to invite you to the wedding reception of their son Aman on 27 October 2012 at Park Hotel in Delhi (Ceremonial Hall on the 1st floor) at 7 p.m.

They look forward to your presence to bless the newly weds.

Best wishes,

Rachna Mehra

d. Invitation issued by the Bride and Groom

Sample:

Sender's Address Line
Date

Dear Akash,

We request the pleasure of your company to our wedding ceremony on 11 October 2012, at the Grand Hotel Banquet Hall at 7 p.m. onwards to celebrate the occasion.

The ceremony will be followed by cocktails and dinner. We hope you will join us on this happy occasion and be a part of our celebrations.

The invitation card is enclosed.

Warm regards,

Raman and Neeta

e. Dinner Invitation Letter

Sample:

Sender's Address Line
Date

Dear Jaya,

Raj and I are having a cocktail and dinner on Saturday 15 September 2013, at 7.30 p.m. at our place. We will be delighted if you and your wife could join us on this occasion.

We are looking forward to a favourable reply from you soon. It would be great opportunity to catch up with you.

Best wishes,

Raj and Sohini

f. Invitation Letter for a Birthday Party

Sample:

Sender's Address Line
Date

Dear Rakhi and Jayant,

It will be a great pleasure if you and your wife could join us at 7.30 p.m. on 13 October 2013, at the Spring Club Lounge on 23, Moira Street, to celebrate Mohan's 50th birthday. Since it is a landmark birthday, I have planned this party as a surprise for him. This is a special occasion and your presence will make it a success.

Looking forward to your confirmation.

Warm regards,

Sheetal

g. Invitation Letter for Cocktails

Sample:

Sender's Address Line
Date

Dear Mohan,

We would be delighted if you and your wife could join us to celebrate a lovely autumn evening with cocktails, followed by a barbeque at our residence from 7 p.m. onwards on 25 October 2013. Since it is an informal party the dress will be casual.

Please confirm by 15 October.

Best wishes,

Murari and Jaya

h. Invitation for a Baby Shower

Sample:

Sender's Address Line
Date

Dear Shubha,

The storks will be visiting us soon and we would like to celebrate the arrival of the baby with our near and dear ones. We are having a baby shower and luncheon on Sunday, 9 September 2013, at 12 noon onwards at our residence. It will be our pleasure if you could join us and give us some words of encouragement and advice to help us to welcome our new baby and share our joy.

Looking forward to seeing you on this happy occasion.

Warm regards,

Maya

i. Acceptance of Dinner Invitation (Formal)

Sample:

Sender's Address Line
Date

Dear Raj and Sohini

Thank you very much for the dinner invitation on 5 October 2013. It will be my pleasure to be present on this occasion.

Warm regards,

Jaya

j. Acceptance of Dinner Invitation (Informal)

Sample:

Date

Dear Sheetal,

Thanks a lot for the invitation and we wouldn't miss it for the world. Both of us would be delighted to come and remind Mohan how he must start acting his age now. But seriously, this is a landmark birthday and we should make it a party to remember.

More when we meet.

Best wishes,

Rakhi

k. Declining an Invitation (formal)

Sample:

Sender's Address Line
Date

Dear Sheetal,

Thank you for the dinner invitation on 9 October 2013. We are sorry we will not be able to attend the dinner due to a prior engagement on that day.

We hope you have a successful party.

Warm regards,

Rita and Milan Menon

l. Declining an Invitation (Informal)

Sample:

Date

Dear Jyoti,

Thank you for the dinner invitation on 9 October 2013. Unfortunately we will not be able to join you as we are going to be away on holiday in Europe. I am sorry we will miss your wonderful cooking, but we must make plans when we return. We hope you have a wonderful party.

Best wishes,

Komal and Rahul

m. Acceptance to a Wedding Invitation

Sender's Address Line
Date

Dear Mr Kalra,

I have received the invitation to your daughter's wedding reception to be held on 3 July 2011. I accept your invitation with great pleasure and it will be my honour to be a part of this special celebration.

Thank you once again for inviting me and please convey my best wishes to your daughter.

Warm regards,

Sohan Arora

4. FESTIVAL GREETINGS LETTERS

These letters are a polite way of wishing friends and relatives during festivals and reminding them that you care. These letters should be short and must convey the essence of the festival.

a. Festival Greetings for Diwali

Sample:

Date
Sender's Address Line

Dear Mita,

Diwali is the festival of lights. On this auspicious occasion, we wish you prosperity, joy, health and wealth. May the glow of the Diwali lights illuminate your days in the year ahead and bring you luck.

Wishing you and your family a very happy Diwali.

Best wishes,

Megha

To: mitaprakash@rediffmail.com
Subject: Happy Diwali

Dear Mita,

Diwali is the festival of lights. On this auspicious occasion, we wish you prosperity, joy, health and wealth. May the glow of the Diwali lights illuminate your days in the year ahead and bring you luck.

Wishing you and your family a very happy Diwali.

Best wishes,

Megha

b. Festival Greetings for Christmas

Sample:

Date
Sender's Address Line

Dear John,

It is the joyful time of the year when we celebrate the birth of Lord Jesus. This is the season to remember family and friends and thank the Lord for showering us with blessings of happiness and good health.

We wish you and yours a very merry Christmas

Best wishes,

Kuntal and Meg

c. Greetings for the New Year

Sample:

Date
Sender's Address Line

Dear Jivan,

We are on the threshold of another year and it's time to bid adieu to 2012 and welcome 2013 with optimism and hope. As the new year flows in, may you be blessed with peace, love and joy. Hope all your dreams and aspirations come true and success comes your way in the new year.

A very happy New Year to you and your family.

Best wishes,

Jiya

d. Festival Greetings for Holi

Sample:

Date
Sender's Address Line

Dear Mahua,

Spring has arrived with a riot of colours, ending the gloom of winter. It is time to welcome the spring with the fun-filled festival of Holi. I hope this Holi is full of happiness for you and your family.

I wish you a very happy Holi replete with colour and fun.

Best wishes,

Kanchan

5. APPRECIATION LETTERS

These letters should be polite and express your gratitude to all those who have helped you out in times of need.

a. Letter of Appreciation for Hospitality

Sample:

Date
Sender's Address Line

Dear Mohan,

It was very nice of you to invite us to spend a week with you. I cannot thank you enough for the wonderful time we had with you. Our stay was most delightful. You and your husband took time off from your busy schedule and accompanied us for sightseeing and we enjoyed every moment of it.

We deeply appreciate your hospitality and we will always treasure every moments of this holiday. We hope you will come and visit us at your convenience so we can have some more good times.

Once again I thank you from the bottom of my heart.

Best wishes,

Jahnavi and Ratan

b. Letter of Appreciation for an Act of Kindness

Sample:

Date
Sender's Address Line

Dear Shantanu,

Thank you so much for your kind assistance. It is really difficult to express my appreciation in mere words. Your kind letter was like a light at the end of a dark tunnel which has guided me in the right direction. In today's world people are so involved with their own lives that they do not bother about other people and you, in spite of being such a busy person, made time for me and tried to resolve my problems. I am touched and overwhelmed by your compassion and thoughtfulness.

You showed me the way to a new beginning when everything looked so bleak and gave me peace of mind.

Please accept my sincere thanks.

Warm regards,

Jayant

To: shantanu.suri@hotmail.com
Subject: Thank You for your Kindness

Dear Shantanu,

Thank you so much for your kind assistance. It is really difficult to express my appreciation in mere words. Your kind letter was like a light at the end of a dark tunnel which has guided me in the right direction. In today's world people are so involved with their own lives that they do not bother about other people and you, in spite of being such a busy person, made time for me and tried to resolve my problems. I am touched and overwhelmed by your compassion and thoughtfulness.

You showed me the way to a new beginning when everything looked so bleak and gave me peace of mind.

Please accept my sincere thanks.

Warm regards,

Jayant

c. Letter of Appreciation for Help while Moving House

Sample:

Date
Sender's Address Line

Dear Ronit,

This is a short note to express my sincere thanks for all your help during the time that we were moving. It was a real back-breaking task moving to a new house after 20 years of living in one place. We could not have managed it so smoothly without your expert help. The packers you arranged for us took care of packing up the entire house in such a methodical way.

Thanks for helping us move and settle into our new house and also assisting us in getting a telephone and gas connection on a priority basis.

Thanks once again.

Warm regards,

Ashok

d. Letter of Appreciation for Financial Help

Sample:

Date
Sender's Address Line

Dear Prakash,

Thank you very much for the generous financial assistance you provided to me during my dire need. This has been a real challenging time in my life and your support has lessened some of my burden. Without your thoughtful act at this point of time, my life could have been very difficult.

I deeply appreciate your kindness and generosity. Thank you once again for being there and extending a helping hand.

Kind regards,

Radheyshyam

6. CONGRATULATIONS LETTERS

There are many happy occasions in life when you need to congratulate your family and friends. These letters should be written immediately after hearing the good news and should be warm and genuine so that they convey your true feelings to the recipients.

An engagement or a wedding is a cause for great celebration. Writing a letter of congratulations gives you an opportunity to express your warm sentiment and to show your happiness for the wedding/engagement. If you could not make it to the wedding or engagement ceremony, it is extremely important to send a letter to express your good wishes. A handwritten letter in simple language with meaningful words is a thoughtful gesture and will be greatly appreciated by the recipients.

a. Congratulations on a Wedding/Engagement

Sample:

Sender's Address Line
Date

Dear Kunal,

Congratulations and best wishes on this wonderful occasion. I am happy to know that you have chosen such an accomplished girl as your life partner and I am sure the two of you will have a long and happy life together.

Your parents told me all about the beautiful ceremony and I am really sorry that I could not see it in person. However, I will definitely come see the two of you soon and all my blessings and good wishes are with you always.

All the best,

Samir and Sahira

b. Congratulations on a Baby

Sample:

Sender's Address Line
Date

Dear Neha,

I am delighted to hear about the arrival of your bundle of joy. Congratulations to both of you on this wonderful occasion.

Both of you must be delighted with the newest addition to your family. It is going to be a very busy and chaotic time, but I am sure that you will enjoy every moment of it.

I wish you all the best in your new role as parents and a very big welcome to the baby in the family. I hope both you and the baby are doing fine.

I wish your whole family a very happy, healthy and prosperous life.

Best wishes,

Ragini

c. Congratulations on a New Job

Sample:

Sender's Address Line
Date

Dear Rakesh,

We are extremely happy to hear about your new appointment as administrative manager of Blue Sky Software Limited. Your appointment does not come as a surprise as a well-qualified person like you deserves the best opportunities in life.

Hope your job opens up new horizons and you progress rapidly in your career.

I know that with your dedication, hard work and acumen, you will be able to climb to the very top of your organization.

We send our heartiest congratulation and best wishes.

Warm wishes,

Sonia and Madhur Scolt

d. Congratulations on Graduating from College

Sample:

Sender's Address Line
Date

Dear Rana,

Congratulations on your splendid achievement. We are proud to know that you are on top of the merit list.

You have always been a brilliant student and this outstanding achievement is the result all your hard work, sincerity and determination.

Congratulations once again and we wish you a very successful and bright future.

Best wishes,

Ram and Priya Sampath

e. Congratulations on Buying a House

Sample:

Sender's Address Line
Date

Dear James,

I am delighted to hear that you have become a proud owner of a beautiful new house.

Shifting from your old house and settling into a new environment involves a lot of work and you must be going through a very hectic time. I have been through the same thing myself and I know that after the first few weeks you will be very comfortable in your new neighbourhood. The new house will be soon become your home which will be filled with laughter and joy.

Congratulations on your purchase and wish you a very happy and memorable stay there.

Best wishes,

Marion and Bob

To: jameswilton@gmail.com
Subject: Congratulations on Buying a New House

Dear James,

I am delighted to hear that you have become a proud owner of a beautiful new house.

Shifting from your old house and settling into a new environment involves a lot of work and you must be going through a very hectic time. I have been through the same thing myself and I know that after the first few weeks you will be very comfortable in your new neighbourhood. The new house will be soon become your home which will be filled with laughter and joy.

Congratulations on your purchase and wish you a very happy and memorable stay there.

Best wishes,

Marion and Bob

f. Congratulations on the Launch of a New Venture

Sample:

Sender's Address Line
Date

Dear Vipul,

I want to take this opportunity to congratulate you on the launch of your new venture.

Starting a new project like this is a really big challenge. The unique conception and the brilliant execution of it is a great achievement. Your new software will be of immense help to the central libraries to categorize their books in no time, which in turn will help the student community to find the required books quickly. The fact that this software can help students access the text remotely through the Internet is a brilliant idea.

Having taught you in the early years of your life, I know that you have a great mind and complete dedication. I am sure that your new venture will be a success and have a great impact on the entire field of library sciences.

I wish you great success and all the best for the future.

Warm wishes,

Professor Venu Madhavan

7. THANK YOU LETTERS

These letters are a symbol of politeness and a token of appreciation for gifts as well as kind gestures by friends and family alike. A thank you letter is always a nice touch after a wedding, birthday party or even a dinner and lets the host know that their efforts were recognized and valued.

a. Thank You for a Wedding Present

Writing thank you letters for a wedding, anniversary, or birthday gift is a way of showing your pleasure and appreciation towards the gifts received. The letter should be simple, thoughtful and must mention why the gift is valued.

Sample:

Sender's Address Line
Date

Dear Radhika,

Thank you very much for attending our wedding reception. I hope you and your husband enjoyed yourselves.

We really loved the gorgeous dinner set you have gifted us. It is an extremely thoughtful gift and perfect for a young couple like us. It is a valuable addition to our new household and we will treasure it always.

Thank you once again for such a wonderful gift.

Warm wishes,

Piyali

To: radhikam@yahoo.com
Subject: Thank You for the Lovely Gift

Dear Radhika,

Thank you very much for attending our wedding reception. I hope you and your husband enjoyed yourselves.

We really loved the gorgeous dinner set you have gifted us. It is an extremely thoughtful gift and perfect for a young couple like us. It is a valuable addition to our new household and we will treasure it always.

Thank you once again for such a wonderful gift.

Warm wishes,

Piyali

b. Thank You for a Birthday Gift

Sample:

Sender's Address Line
Date

Dear Megha,

Thank you for coming to my birthday party. Your presence meant a lot to me and made the evening more special. The beautiful Fab India vase you gave me is a perfect addition to my living room and matches the rest of our decor beautifully.

Thank you once again for coming and for your thoughtful gift.

Warmly,

Neeta

c. Thank You for a Dinner Party

Sample:

Sender's Address Line
Date

Dear Radha,

Thank you so much for the wonderful dinner party that you hosted last night. It was such a wonderful evening and we had a lovely time meeting all your friends who were a very interesting group of people.

The food was amazing and the wine was marvellous. In short, it was a lovely party and both Jahan and I had a fabulous time.

Thanks once again for your kind invitation.

With love,

Sonali and Jahan

8. ACKNOWLEDGEMENT LETTERS

An acknowledgement letter can convey appreciation of support or timely services provided by a person or group. The positive effects of the action should be mentioned in a sincere way. The letter should be courteous, simple, brief and prompt. Acknowledgement can relate to various topics:

- Emotional support
- Delivery of goods and services
- Payment
- Social service
- Donations

a. Acknowledgement of Timely Delivery of Goods

Sample:

Sender's Address Line
Date

Dear Mr Kakar,

I would like to thank you for the prompt delivery of the washing machine that I had ordered through your online catalogue and your company's after-sales service. The machine was delivered and installed three days of my booking it. I appreciate the effort you have put in for the benefit of your customers and I hope this trend will continue.

Thank you for the good work.

Warm regards,

Aban Ray

b. Acknowledgement for Emotional support

Acknowledging emotional support is the best way to convey your thanks and let the addressee know that you really appreciate the effort that he or she put in to comfort you in your hour of need. This is a personal and informal letter and should be written simply and honestly.

Sample:

Sender's Address Line
Date

Dear Amrit,

Thank you very much for your support after I lost my job last month. As both a friend and colleague, you have been more than kind and your cheerful letters and phone calls inspired me and boosted my morale.

At your advice, I stopped sitting around the house feeling depressed, and started job hunting with a new vigour. You will be happy to know that I have just been employed by Electronics Limited as their General Manager (Projects).

I cannot express enough how much your support meant to me. It has helped me pull myself together and renew my confidence in myself.

Thank you once again.

Faithfully,

Nimesh

9. GET WELL LETTERS

These letters should be upbeat and cheerful and should put across your concern and good will. These letters are sent to people suffering from an illness, or to those who have been hospitalized due to an accident, or for treatment. Handwritten letters are better than cards as they carry a personal touch.

Sample:

Sender's Address Line
Date

Dear Kiran,

We came to know recently that you are not keeping well and going to be hospitalized for treatment. We hope you get well soon. You are a very special friend to all of us in our ladies' kitty group and we want to see you fit and fine soon.

We are sending all our best wishes for your speedy recovery and good health.

Please let us know when we can come visit you. We will be in touch with your husband and will call him before we come to see you in hospital.

With best wishes,

Manisha Jindal
Behala Kitty Group Secretary

10. CONDOLENCE LETTERS

Condolence letters offer great comfort to someone who is mourning the loss of their loved ones. It serves as a tribute to the deceased and conveys sympathy and support. Your compassion is transmitted into words and the letter simply shows your support at the hour of need. Keep it brief and simple and put in a few good words about the deceased person.

a. Condolence on the Death of a Friend/Relative's Parent

Sample:

Date

Dear Mohua,

I was truly sad to hear about the death of your mother. I know you are going through a very difficult phase of your life. Losing a parent is always a traumatic experience for the children and I understand your pain. Your mother was such a gentle soul and was always ready to help others with a big smile. When I lost my mother she was always there to console me. I will always remember her as a most loving person and her ever-ready smile will always be missed.

May God bless you and give you the strength to go through this loss.

Faithfully,

Nina

To: mohuamari@gmail.com
Subject: Condolences

Dear Mohua,

I was truly sad to hear about the death of your mother. I know you are going through a very difficult phase of your life. Losing a parent is always a traumatic experience for the children and I understand your pain. Your mother was such a gentle soul and was always ready to help others with a big smile. When I lost my mother she was always there to console me. I will always remember her as a most loving person and her ever-ready smile will always be missed.

May God bless you and give you the strength to go through this loss.

Faithfully,

Nina

b. Condolence on the Death of a Colleague's Parent

Sample:

Sender's Address Line
Date

Dear Roop,

We are sorry to hear of your father's sad demise. It was such an untimely death and has saddened everyone.

He was a remarkable person and will be fondly remembered by all. He was an outstanding entrepreneur and a thorough gentleman. I had met him on a few occasions and will always treasure the moments I spent with him. He was an example of a model businessman and a source of inspiration to all his employees.

Please accept my deepest condolences on this sad occasion.

May his soul rest in peace.

Yours sincerely,

Suparn Modak

c. Condolence on the Death of a Relative/Friend's Child

Sample:

Dear Mugdha,

There is no pain deeper than losing a child. Words are inadequate to express the sorrow and pain that you are going through. Our thoughts are with you during this terrible time. We are finding this shocking news very difficult to accept and we can't even begin to imagine your loss. No one can take your pain away. We only hope that you find some comfort thinking that she is now in a better place.

Sania was such an angel and will always be missed by her loved ones.

All our wishes are with you.

Faithfully,

Suraj and Naina

d. Condolence on the Death of a Colleague's Child

Sample:

Sender's Address Line
Date

Dear Mr Kapoor,

We are shocked to hear about your loss. Robin was such a wonderful child and he will always be missed terrible by everybody who knew him.

Please accept our heartfelt condolences to you and your family. Life is sometime so unfair – losing someone as young and lively as Robin is really tragic.

May God give you strength to get through this difficult time.

Yours sincerely,

Mohan Saini

e. Condolence on the Death of a Friend's Spouse

Sample:

Dear Raj,

I am so sorry to hear the news of Raman's death. It is really hard to believe the news. My thoughts are with you and I can imagine the intensity of your pain.

Raman was such a wonderful human being and he will be always missed by all who came in contact with him. He was always extending a helping hand to people who were in trouble and was the life of every party.

In spite of the prolonged illness, it is difficult to accept that he is no more. The thought that his agony is over and he is in a better place may comfort you somehow. Now you can think of him as a healthy and cheerful person as he was before his sickness

We are always with you at this hour of grief.

Fondly,

Meera and Kumar

f. Condolence on the Death of a Friend's Pet

Losing a pet is no less significant than losing a family member. For a pet lover, a pet becomes a part of the family and the death of a pet causes the same heartbreak and pain to the owner as the loss of a person.

Sample:

Date

Dear Chanda,

I am so sorry to hear of your dog, Billy's death. Billy was an important part of your household and it will take some time for you to go through life without her lively presence. She was a real bundle of joy. I still remember the day when you brought her home – you were so excited and she looked like a fluffy ball. Someone very correctly said that dogs are not our whole life but they make our life whole.

Please accept my deepest sympathy.

With love,

Lynne

g. Condolence on a Miscarriage

A miscarriage is an irreparable loss for the couple. From the day of the conception, the parents eagerly look forward to the birth of their child. It is very painful to accept that there will be no birth to celebrate. In such a situation it is better to send a few lines to express your sorrow after a few days.

Sample:

Date

Dear Rina,

We are really sad to hear about your wife's miscarriage. We are always with you in your moment of grief. May God give you strength to go through this difficult time.

Faithfully,

Ritika

h. Condolence on a Stillborn

The pain of parents of a stillborn child is unbearable. A few sincere words somehow provide some comfort in their time of sadness.

Sample:

Date

Dear Sunita,

We are shocked to hear the news that the baby visited this earth only a few moments before he departed for his heavenly abode. We are sorry for the deep anguish and pain you are going through. We pray to God that he blesses you with peace of mind.

We send us all our love and you are always in our thoughts.

Yours faithfully,

Megha

11. SYMPATHY LETTERS

There are moments in life when unforeseen events leave people shattered and in need of emotional support. The basic object of a sympathy letter is to express your concern and offer your help and support. The tone of the letter should be positive and cheerful so that it brightens up the recipient's mood.

a. Sympathy Letter for an Accident

Sample:

Sender's Address Line
Date

Dear Mr Patel,

I am sorry to hear about your accident. I was quite surprised when I heard that your car collided with another car as you are such a cautious driver and usually have excellent control over the wheels. I hope your injuries are not too bad and that you bounce back on your feet in no time.

Wish you a speedy recovery. I will visit you next week only if you are up to receiving visitors. I will call your wife to find out the details of visiting hours.

Take care and see you back home soon.

Best wishes,

Mohan Menon

b. Sympathy Letter for a Divorce

Couples going through a divorce face a lot of hardships, both emotional and financial. It is not only a legal procedure but a time of great emotional upheaval. Friends and family need to come together to support and comfort them to go through this trauma. A line or two in sympathy will bring some kind of solace to them.

Sample:

Date

Dear Sita,

We are truly sorry to know that you and your husband have parted ways. Please remember that we are with you during this difficult and trying time. I hope we can do something to lessen your pain.

I know that it takes a great deal of strength to go through the ordeal of divorce. You are a mature and strong person and I'm sure that you will be able to get through this with your positive attitude.

Please let us know if we can be of any help to you.

With love,

Minu

c. Sympathy Letter on Retrenchment

These letters should be encouraging and try to boost the morale of a person who is feeling depressed and low after losing a job.

When a situation feels hopeless and the future looks grim, a sincere sympathy letter provides encouragement and can give hope and courage.

Sample:

Date

Dear Rohan,

I am sorry to hear the disappointing news. Please do not think it happened due to any shortcomings on your side as the present economic conditions have made this almost a daily occurrence with a number of MNCs in our country. I am writing to you because I can understand what you are going through. I faced a similar situation in the early days of my career. I was young and dispensable and was fired without a thought. Even if the financial recession is alarming and hundreds of people are losing their jobs, things are bound to improve soon.

You have to focus on the positive side and make the best of the situation. With your experience and qualifications you can start a consultancy agency and provide technological knowhow to smaller companies. After massive retrenchment, most of the companies will look towards technical outsourcing. At the beginning it might be little tough but consider that teething trouble. I am quite certain that with your sincerity, hard work and determination, success will come to your ultimately.

Please let me know if I can be of any help and do call me if you want to discuss anything.

Best wishes,

Manmohan Uncle

d. Sympathy Letter to a Friend who has Filed for Bankruptcy

It is a very difficult time for a person going through bankruptcy. This particular letter should be written in a very sensitive way to provide emotional support without criticizing his or her actions. The letter should try to inspire the person and encourage him to try to take things in his stride.

Sample:

Sender's Address Line
Date

Dear Mr Kumar,

I just heard the sad news that you are going through financial hardships and had to close down your business. The present economic recession is responsible to a great extent for this situation. Most of the small business concerns are struggling to barely stay afloat. I know you started your winery with much hope and aspirations and the wines you produced were among the best in India. However, it was perhaps ahead of its times.

Please remember that bankruptcy is not the end of the world. Your optimistic and confident approach towards life will help you to overcome this problem. I am sure you can manage to streamline and reorganize the business once more when the time is right. Please always remember the greater the struggle, the more magnificent is the triumph.

Please let me know if I can be of any assistance in any way.

Best wishes,

Mrityunjoy Lahiri

To: milan.kumar@yahooindia.com
Subject: Sympathy letter

Dear Mr Kumar,

I just heard the sad news that you are going through financial hardships and had to close down your business. The present economic recession is responsible to a great extent for this situation. Most of the small business concerns are struggling to barely stay afloat. I know you started your winery with much hope and aspirations and the wines you produced were among the best in India. However, it was perhaps ahead of its times.

Please remember that bankruptcy is not the end of the world. Your optimistic and confident approach towards life will help you to overcome this problem. I am sure you can manage to streamline and reorganize the business once more when the time is right. Please always remember the greater the struggle, the more magnificent is the triumph.

Please let me know if I can be of any assistance in any way.

Best wishes,

Mrityunjoy Lahiri

12. APOLOGY LETTERS

Apology letters should be written as soon as possible after any untoward situation or incident. A sincere apology letter helps to ease the tension and to some extent sort out the problem. This kind of letter should express sincere regret. The letter should start with an apology and explain the matter clearly. It should also mention the corrective steps to resolve the problem if possible. These letters can be personal as well as formal.

Formal Apology Letters

The ideal Formal Apology Letter is written in a professional and polite manner. The key word of this letter is to acknowledge the mistake and accept responsibility for it. A timely written apology letter can help to a great extent to rectify the situation and improve the relationship between the sender and the addressee.

Personal Apology Letters

These are informal letters, usually written to relatives or friends for unpleasant encounters or inadvertent mistakes. Acknowledging a mistake and apologizing for it makes things easier and paves the way for an amicable solution of the problem.

a. Formal Apology Letter for Not Attending Interview

Sample:

Sender's Address Line
Phone Number/Email address
Date

Dear Sir,

I sincerely apologize for not attending the interview with your company on 19 June 2013. The interview letter was delivered to my residence on 18 June 2013, and it was too late for me to rearrange my schedule.

As I had had no prior intimation about the interview, I had planned a trip out of station with my family for five days and by the time I got the letter, it was too late to reschedule. We were leaving the house on 18 June itself when the letter arrived.

I regret that I could not meet you for further discussion about potential employment in your company. I hope another interview may be arranged at your convenience. Please give me seven days notice and if possible, please notify me on my mobile phone as my present job requires me to travel quite a bit. My cell number is mentioned on the top of the letter.

I trust my absence from the interview will not impart any negative feelings. I am looking forward to meeting you shortly.

Kind regards,

Signature

Rukhsana Adil

b Formal Apology Letter to a Customer for Wrong delivery of Goods

Sample:

Sender's Address Line
Phone Number/Email address
Date

Dear Sir,

Please accept my sincere apology for the wrong delivery of your reference books. I genuinely regret the inconvenience caused to you. I will have a representative pick up the wrong books and send you a fresh package as soon as possible.

Our company's goal is to serve the customers to the best of our ability and as I personally came to your house and took your order, there should have been no confusion.

We normally never make mistakes like this. Although there is no excuse for such a mix-up, I just wanted to let you know that our office has relocated to a new address recently and the computer systems are still being set up and that is why somehow your orders got interchanged with another one.

I have personally overseen and dispatched your consignment and it should reach you this evening or tomorrow morning at the latest.

I am really sorry for the inconvenience caused to you.

Warm regards,

Signature

Sontu Ghosh

Personal Apology Letter to a Friend for Bad Behaviour at a Party

Sample:

Date

Dear Kunal,

Please accept my sincere apology for the embarrassment and pain I caused to you yesterday at your birthday party. It was a great party and I think I had a little too much to drink. Although that is no justification for my behaviour, I wanted to let you know that I would normally never let an argument go that far.

I admit I was wrong and am truly sorry for creating such a scene. My remarks were totally out of context and unwarranted in such a social gathering which also included your colleagues from work.

Please excuse the behaviour of a drunk man and I hope we can put this incident behind us and even laugh about it some day.

Sorry once again.

Warm regards,

Manoj

To: kunalk@gmail.com
Subject: Apology

Dear Kunal,

Please accept my sincere apology for the embarrassment and pain I caused to you yesterday at your birthday party. It was a great party and I think I had a little too much to drink. Although that is no justification for my behaviour, I wanted to let you know that I would normally never let an argument go that far.

I admit I was wrong and am truly sorry for creating such a scene. My remarks were totally out of context and unwarranted in such a social gathering which also included your colleagues from work.

Please excuse the behaviour of a drunk man and I hope we can put this incident behind us and even laugh about it some day.

Sorry once again.

Warm regards,

Manoj

13. LETTERS GIVING ADVICE

These type of letters are usually written by professionals and competent people who are able to impart genuine advice. They can be formal or informal depending on the topic and the nature of the relationship with the addressee. The purpose of the letter should be clear and understanding. It should provide:

- Required guidance on the topic
- No excessive advice
- It should be balanced

a. Advice on a New Job from a Friend who is a Guidance Counsellor

Sample:

Date

Dear Deepak,

The last few months have not been going well in your work place and I know that it has been affecting your peace of mind and making you feel depressed. Please do not lose faith in yourself. Do remember that every cloud has a silver lining and better times will eventually come in your life, so do not feel bitter or lonely.

If you want to take a bold step, first you need to believe in yourself and justify your action whether it relates to a job or a relationship.

First you need to assess your current job and see what is going wrong. Then if you do decide to take a new job, things should be considered in a proper perspective. The salary should not be the only criteria. Please take into account the other prerequisites such as medical benefits, superannuation and the location of the job. If the new job entails relocation, please weigh the advantages and disadvantages of shifting. After due consideration if you feel like a new opportunity is going to open doors for you, please do take this step.

It would be best if you take your time to make the right decision. If you need any suggestions or advice from me, please do not hesitate to get in touch.

All my best wishes for a better future.

Yours sincerely,

Mandy Puri

b. Legal Advice Letter

Sample:

Sender's Address Line
Phone Number/Email address
Date

Dear Mr Kumar,

Thank you for seeking my professional advice. I have given some guidelines which will help you to solve your problem.

I have received all the papers related to this case. Based on my understanding of the matter, my suggestion is that you file your claim in the Court of Small Causes after paying the requisite court fees.

You should have all your facts right and the paperwork in order to prove your claim. In this particular case you do not need a lawyer and just a dossier of evidence will suffice.

However, if you feel that during the hearing you might have difficulty to prove your points, please let me know well in advance and I will be there to provide you with the legal assistance.

Yours sincerely,

Signature

Kumud Mohanty

14. LETTERS BETWEEN LANDLORD AND TENANTS

These letters must be carefully drafted as small arguments and differences could lead to a termination of a contract between the two parties. Also in case any dispute arises, these letters could be used as evidence or result in undue payment of large sums of money. It is better to send these letters as hard copies as they will carry greater weight in a court of law.

a. Apology to Landlord for Late Payment of Rent

Sample:

Sender's Address Line
Phone Number/Email address
Date

Mr R.S. Seth
2nd Floor
Suraj Apartment
25, Airport Road
Bangalore – 560 022

Dear Sir,

I sincerely apologize for late payment of rent for the month of May 2013, which was due on 5 June.

My business is presently going through a bit of a financial crunch as the payment from some of my larger clients including the Government of Karnataka have been held up due to the upcoming elections. I have had to liquidize a lot of my assets to make the other payments required to run my business.

I am enclosing the rent cheque along with the late payment fee as per our rent agreement.

Once again, I apologize for the inconvenience caused by my late payment and I thank you for your understanding and patience. I also assure you that this will not happen again.

Thanking you,

Signature

Hitesh Mahajan

b. Warning Letter to Tenant Reminding him about Late Payment of Rent

Sample:

Sender's Address Line
Phone Number/Email address
Date

Mr Atish Dikshit
Flat No 3B
Akash Bhavan
25, Anna Salai
Chennai – 600 002

Dear Sir,

This is to inform you that the rent for Flat no 3B, Akash Bhavan, has been outstanding for the last three months have been outstanding and despite my continued reminders, there has been no response from your end. According to the rent agreement executed on 1 April 2013, the rent has to be paid by the 4th of each month.

I have noted that from the first month itself you have been paying rent as late as 15th of the month without showing any valid reason. Although I have been understanding and not paid too much heed to this, now the amount has become too large for me to excuse it.

From this month onward you will be charged a late fee of ₹ 500 per day after 4th of the month till you pay the rent.

In future if the situation does not improve, or you fail to deposit the outstanding rent within a week of this letter, I shall have no other option but to terminate the rent agreement and issue an eviction notice thereafter.

I sincerely hope that to avoid any further unpleasantness, you will take urgent steps to clear your dues with immediate effect and regularize your future payments.

Yours faithfully,

Signature

Amrit Trivedi

c. Complaint Letter to Tenant regarding Maintenance of the House

Sample:

Sender's Address Line
Phone Number/Email address
Date

Mr Rajan Yadav
238, Central Avenue
Flat No 2B
Mandakini Apartment
Kolkata – 700 013

Dear Sir,

During a recent visit by my representative it was found that the flat is in a terrible state. As per the tenancy agreement you are supposed to maintain the cleanliness of the house. The flat was handed over to you in a spick and span condition and as per the terms, you are obliged to maintain it in that condition excepting the normal wear and tear.

You have defaced the wall by putting nails at random and as a result, the plaster and paint have been chipped off at number of places. Window panes are broken and the walls have got damp marks. The compound is littered with garbage although there is a garbage disposal system in the building.

Your children have put stickers on main door as well as the inside doors thereby spoiling the polish.

Please make it a point to keep the flat in a good condition. I understand with children around it is not always possible, but then you have to make an extra effort to restore it to the original condition.

Hope you will do the needful under the circumstances without any further reminder from me.

Thanking you,

Signature

Manoj Shah

d. Complaint Letter to Landlord regarding Maintenance of the House

Sample:

Sender's Address Line
Phone Number/Email address
Date

Mr Madhur Karlekar
Flat No. 3A
332, Andheri West
Mumbai – 400 025

Dear Sir,

I had moved into your flat (Flat 4B, 332, Andheri West) on rent on 1 July 2012, for three years. As per the Tenancy Agreement executed between us, you are supposed to carry out annual maintenance work to keep the house in good condition.

I am sorry to point out that in the last year nothing has been done. The roof over the corridor has been leaking whenever it rains. There is seepage of water in the bathroom and consequently the walls have become damp. The paint has started chipping from the damp portions and it needs urgent repair work.

I have informed you repeatedly over the phone to start the maintenance work before the monsoon sets in, but so far nothing has been done. Living in a damp atmosphere is causing lot of health problems for me and my family. We are going through lot of inconvenience.

I would appreciate your immediate action.

Yours faithfully,

Signature

Jayant Saxena

e. Letter to Tenant Questioning Structural Changes to the Property

Sample:

Sender's Address Line
Phone Number/Email address
Date

Mr Manohar Arya
1499, Wind Tunnel Road
Bangalore – 560 034

Dear Sir,

It is with regret that I wish to apprise you of certain violations of the terms of Tenancy Agreement executed between us. You have carried out unauthorized structural alterations to the property occupied by you. You will appreciate that no alteration/renovation should have been carried out without prior permission from me. My representative during the last visit noted that you had partitioned the living room by building a wall and an extra room.

In the interest of maintaining a cordial relationship, you are requested to get the altered portion immediately restored to the original status. You are also advised to refrain from carrying out any renovations/alteration without permission from me in the future, failing which I will be forced to take legal action in the matter.

Yours faithfully,

Signature

Avinash Daga

15. TRAVEL LETTERS

These letters are important as they communicate one's travel itinerary and plans. These letters should be clear and dates, timings and preferences should be double checked as they will influence the nature of the holiday. These letters should mention the following:

- Dates
- Duration
- Timing
- Flight details

a. Letter Booking Travel Package from an Online Travel Portal

Sample:

Sender's Address Line
Phone Number/Email address
Date

Mr Arpan Singh
Indiawidetours.com
1529, Brabourne Road
Kolkata – 700 001

Dear Mr Singh,

Your attractive advertisement for the package tour to Kashmir (for eleven nights and 10 days costing ₹ 35,000 per head) sounds quite interesting. Your email stated that this tour will cover all major tourist spots and include a three-star hotel stay with transport.

After going through your website I have got all the required information and I would like to book my wife and myself for the upcoming tour on 5 November 2013. I have filled in the particulars needed by you for registration.

Once you confirm our registration, I will make the necessary payments.

Looking forward for an early confirmation from your end.

Thanking you,

Rohit Rai

b. Letter Booking a Hotel Room

Sample:

Sender's Address Line
Phone Number/Email address
Date

Greenfield Hotel
Reservation Center
22, Hosur Road
Bangalore – 560 067

Dear Sir,

I would like to book a deluxe room for 3 days from 25 July to 28 July 2013 in my name. I will reach on 25th morning from Delhi by the Air Konnect flight no AK 242 at 9 a.m. I would also like to avail of your airport pick-up service.

I am couriering this letter for speedy confirmation and while confirming my booking, please send me the best rates you can offer for the period mentioned. If any advance payment is required, please indicate that in the mail and I will arrange to remit it immediately.

Your prompt action will be highly appreciated.

Thanking you,

Rehan Bansal

c. Cancellation of Hotel Reservation

Sample:

Sender's Address Line
Phone Number/Email address
Date

Greenfield Hotel
Reservation Center
22, Hosur Road
Bangalore – 560 067

Dear Sir,

This has reference to my letter dated 7 July 2013 booking a deluxe room from 25 July to 28 July 2013.

As my trip has been cancelled, I would request you to cancel the above reservation against my name.

Please arrange to remit the advance amount paid by me against the reservation at an early date after deducting the necessary charges as applicable according to your terms and conditions.

Thanking you,

Rehan Bansal

16. GOODBYE LETTERS

These letters should have a personal touch and even if it is a group mail, it should make each reader feel like they were special in your life. Try and address each individual or family by their name when sending a goodbye letter as that makes all the difference.

a. Goodbye Letter to Neighbours and Friends

Sample:

Sender's Address Line
Phone Number/Email address
Date

Raj Kiran Rao
Villa no 122
Palm Meadows
Ramagondanahalli
Bangalore – 560028

Dear Raj,

I am writing this mail with a heavy heart to bid goodbye to you and your family as I have been transferred to Kolkata. We are planning to leave by the end of this month as my joining date in the Kolkata office is 1 August 2013.

I remember the first day in this community when we were apprehensive about our welcome as we were outsiders. But the way you welcomed me and my family into your lives and social circle helped us settle in with great ease. Our time here felt like we were a part of an extended family.

I will miss our weekend get-togethers and other social activities during festivals. We had a wonderful time enjoying your hospitality.

Thanks to you for your support and warm friendship during my stay here. My best wishes to you and your own.

I will get in touch with you as soon as I settle down and in the meantime please stay in touch through email.

Warm regards,

Rishav Dutt

17. COMPLAINT LETTERS TO NEIGHBOURS

These letters should be polite yet firm and detail the nature of the complaint and point out why it is an inconvenience to you. It should also mention the corrective measures required from the neighbour's end.

a. Complaint Letter to Neighbour regarding Damage to Shared Water Pump

Sample:

Sender's Address Line
Phone Number/Email address
Date

Mr Avinash Mishra
Flat no 1A
3535, Park Street
Kolkata – 700 016

Dear Sir,

Recently, you had carried out extensive repair work to your water pipeline and your plumber unintentionally damaged the main pipe connected to water pump in the process. As a result, it has affected our water supply and we are not getting our quota of water from the municipal corporation. In fact, the water comes in as a trickle every morning and evening and it is causing us distress. We called our plumber to take a look at the pipes and he said that the main pipe has got blocked while repairing it.

I would request you to please ask your plumber to come take a look and rectify the problem so that the normal water supply is restored. This matter needs your urgent attention and your early action will be highly appreciated.

Thanking you,

Ramesh Deo

b. Complaint Letter to Neighbour regarding their Dog Dirtying the Compound

Sample:

Sender's Address Line
Phone Number/Email address
Date

Mr Amish Dheer
Flat no 3B
Moonlight Apartments
23, Old Airport Road
Bangalore – 560017

Dear Sir,

May I draw your attention to the fact that your dog is dirtying the compound every morning. In spite of frequent verbal complaints, I regret to state that no action has been taken by you to rectify the situation.

As a pet owner you are responsible for your dog's actions and ensure that he does not cause a nuisance and inconvenience to the neighbours. Dog droppings are unsightly and unpleasant. You are supposed to clean up after the dog dirties up the common passage and dispose of it in a suitable manner. A dirty passage pollutes the whole environment and we are many families who are facing this issue because of your dog.

We have discussed this issue several times in the recent past but without any result. Please help us to keep our compound clean and healthy for our children to play in.

Thanking you in anticipation.

Yours faithfully,

Randheer Garg

Secretary
Moonlight Owners Association

c. Complaint Letter to Resident's Welfare Association regarding Timely Collection of Garbage

Sample:

Sender's Address Line
Phone Number/Email address
Date

Secretary
Blue Valley Residents' Association
Saket
New Delhi – 110017

Dear Sir,

I seek to draw your immediate attention to the fact that the garbage collection system has become very slack. Residents have complained to you on several occasions, but so far no steps have been taken to regularize timely collection of garbage from our homes.

I have been living in this complex for the last 10 years and always enjoyed the excellent service of the maintenance crew. Unfortunately in recent times the service has become unsatisfactory and it is going from bad to worse everyday. The current staff who are in charge of collecting garbage appear to be careless in their work. They come at all odd times and work in a very slipshod manner leaving a trail of garbage behind them. Also people who have to go out for work, leave their garbage outside their doors and it sits there for hours before being collected. This is making the complex dirty and polluting the environment and could cause a health hazard to all.

We would appreciate your urgent action in the matter.

Thanking you,

Raj Kiran Rao

9789350097649